PRAISE FOR M. L. BUCHMAN

A fabulous soaring thriller.

> — *TAKE OVER AT MIDNIGHT*, MIDWEST BOOK REVIEW

Meticulously researched, hard-hitting, and suspenseful.

> — *PURE HEAT*, PUBLISHERS WEEKLY, STARRED REVIEW

Expert technical details abound, as do realistic military missions with superb imagery that will have readers feeling as if they are right there in the midst and on the edges of their seats.

> — *LIGHT UP THE NIGHT*, RT REVIEWS, 4 1/2 STARS

Buchman has catapulted his way to the top tier of my favorite authors.

> — FRESH FICTION

Nonstop action that will keep readers on the edge of their seats.

> — *TAKE OVER AT MIDNIGHT,* LIBRARY JOURNAL

M L. Buchman's ability to keep the reader right in the middle of the action is amazing.

> — LONG AND SHORT REVIEWS

The only thing you'll ask yourself is, "When does the next one come out?"

> — *WAIT UNTIL MIDNIGHT,* RT REVIEWS, 4 STARS

The first...of (a) stellar, long-running (military) romantic suspense series.

> — *THE NIGHT IS MINE,* BOOKLIST, "THE 20 BEST ROMANTIC SUSPENSE NOVELS: MODERN MASTERPIECES"

I knew the books would be good, but I didn't realize how good.

> — NIGHT STALKERS SERIES, KIRKUS REVIEWS

Buchman mixes adrenalin-spiking battles and brusque military jargon with a sensitive approach.

— PUBLISHERS WEEKLY

13 times "Top Pick of the Month"

— NIGHT OWL REVIEWS

Tom Clancy fans open to a strong female lead will clamor for more.

— *DRONE*, PUBLISHERS WEEKLY

Superb! Miranda is utterly compelling!

— *BOOKLIST,* STARRED REVIEW

Miranda Chase continues to astound and charm.

— BARB M.

Escape Rating: A. Five Stars! OMG just start with *Drone* and be prepared for a fantastic binge-read!

— READING REALITY

The best military thriller I've read in a very long time. Love the female characters.

— *DRONE,* SHELDON MCARTHUR,
FOUNDER OF THE MYSTERY
BOOKSTORE, LA

BEYOND PRINCE CHARMING

ONE GUY'S GUIDE TO WRITING MEN IN
ROMANCE (AND BEYOND)

STRATEGIES FOR SUCCESS
BOOK 5

M. L. BUCHMAN

Copyright 2023 Matthew L. Buchman

All rights reserved.

This book, or parts thereof, may not be reproduced in any form without permission from the author.

Receive a free book and discover more by this author at: www.mlbuchman.com

Cover images:

Training © kbuntu

SIGN UP FOR M. L. BUCHMAN'S NEWSLETTER TODAY

and receive:
Release News
Free Short Stories
a Free Book

Get your free book today. Do it now.
free-book.mlbuchman.com

CONTENTS

Also by M. L. Buchman	xi
About This Book	xiii
My Thanks	xv

THE INTRODUCTORY BITS

Beginnings	3

PART I
A BASIS TO BUILD FROM

1. The Other Shoe	13
2. Researching: Dartan's Story	18
3. Time-frame-driven Point of View	22
4. The Author's Voice	25
5. Fallacies	29

PART II
GUY-SPEAK

6. The Kiss	41
7. Extreme Guy-speak	46
8. Some Examples	51
9. The "Voice"	56
10. A Few Final Guy-Speak Thoughts	60
11. Another Final Guy-Speak Thought	64
12. Guy Voice	66

PART III
PHYSICALITY

13. Athletics	73
14. Programming	77
15. The Man's Body	84
16. The Fighting Man	92

17. Reaction Types	97
18. The DNA of Sex	100

PART IV
RELATIONSHIPS

19. The Why	107
20. Who Chases Who	112
21. At Battle	115
22. The Weeping Woman	120

PART V
THE JOURNEY

23. The Hero's Journey	125
24. The Modern Hero's Journey	133

PART VI
THE FINAL BITS

25. Men in Romance	139
OTHER STRATEGIES FOR SUCCESS TITLES	143
About the Author	149
Also by M. L. Buchman	151
Sign up for M. L. Buchman's newsletter today	153

Other works by M. L. Buchman: *(* - also in audio)*

Action-Adventure Thrillers

Dead Chef
One Chef!
Two Chef!

Miranda Chase
Drone*
Thunderbolt*
Condor*
Ghostrider*
Raider*
Chinook*
Havoc*
White Top*
Start the Chase*
Lightning*
Skibird*
Nightwatch*
Osprey*
Gryphon*

Science Fiction / Fantasy

Deities Anonymous
Cookbook from Hell: Reheated
Saviors 101

Contemporary Romance

Eagle Cove
Return to Eagle Cove
Recipe for Eagle Cove
Longing for Eagle Cove
Keepsake for Eagle Cove

Love Abroad
Heart of the Cotswolds: England
Path of Love: Cinque Terre, Italy

Where Dreams
Where Dreams are Born
Where Dreams Reside
Where Dreams Are of Christmas*
Where Dreams Unfold
Where Dreams Are Written
Where Dreams Continue

Non-Fiction

Strategies for Success
Managing Your Inner Artist/Writer
Estate Planning for Authors*
Character Voice
Narrate and Record Your Own Audiobook*

Short Story Series by M. L. Buchman:

Action-Adventure Thrillers

Dead Chef

Miranda Chase Stories

Romantic Suspense

Antarctic Ice Fliers

US Coast Guard

Contemporary Romance

Eagle Cove

Other

Deities Anonymous (fantasy)

Single Titles

The Emily Beale Universe
(military romantic suspense)

The Night Stalkers
MAIN FLIGHT
The Night Is Mine
I Own the Dawn
Wait Until Dark
Take Over at Midnight
Light Up the Night
Bring On the Dusk
By Break of Day
Target of the Heart
Target Lock on Love
Target of Mine
Target of One's Own
NIGHT STALKERS HOLIDAYS
Daniel's Christmas*
Frank's Independence Day*
Peter's Christmas*
Christmas at Steel Beach
Zachary's Christmas*
Roy's Independence Day*
Damien's Christmas*
Christmas at Peleliu Cove

Henderson's Ranch
Nathan's Big Sky*
Big Sky, Loyal Heart*
Big Sky Dog Whisperer*
Tales of Henderson's Ranch*

Shadow Force: Psi
At the Slightest Sound*
At the Quietest Word*
At the Merest Glance*
At the Clearest Sensation*

White House Protection Force
Off the Leash*
On Your Mark*
In the Weeds*

Firehawks
Pure Heat
Full Blaze
Hot Point*
Flash of Fire*
Wild Fire

SMOKEJUMPERS
Wildfire at Dawn*
Wildfire at Larch Creek*
Wildfire on the Skagit*

Delta Force
Target Engaged*
Heart Strike*
Wild Justice*
Midnight Trust*

Emily Beale Universe Short Story Series
The Night Stalkers
The Night Stalkers Stories
The Night Stalkers CSAR
The Night Stalkers Wedding Stories
The Future Night Stalkers

Delta Force
Th Delta Force Shooters
The Delta Force Warriors

Firehawks
The Firehawks Lookouts
The Firehawks Hotshots
The Firebirds

White House Protection Force
Stories

Future Night Stalkers
Stories (Science Fiction)

ABOUT THIS BOOK

Why are men so often clichés on the romantic page? They don't need to be. Not even when real-life men appear to be clichés of themselves. These techniques can create male characters who pop off the page in any genre for their realism and depth.

Come join the male author of over a hundred short stories and fifty romance novels and twenty thrillers (including numerous Top 10 Romance of the Year accolades from B&N, NPR, and various industry reviewers) as he explores: common tropes (and why they're wrong even when they're so right), guy-speak, emotions, physicality, journeys, and much more.

Also we'll tackle the Kinda-Myths: grunting, silent, brooding, uncommunicative, punching walls, rampant sex drive (while in a gunfight), arrogance, lack of emotion, conversations all about them...

MY THANKS

As always, there is an awesome team behind me, but I needed their assistance more than ever to bring this book to life.

My two anonymous alpha readers, you totally rock! They're the ones who knocked my ramblings into a comprehensible form.

Colleen my wizard proofreader who actually went through this book twice for me due to late changes.

My thanks to RWA University who lit the spark by asking me to teach a two-hour class on Writing Men in Romance.

And the professional and beyond awesome Millennial beta-reader who helped me be age considerate / inclusive (remaining foibles are mine): Evelyn Hyde at https://madamehyde.carrd.co/

My thanks all.

THE INTRODUCTORY BITS

BEGINNINGS

Obligatory (brief) "Why Listen to Me" Section

I HAD A CONVOLUTED INTRODUCTION TO WRITING MEN. It came in many phases, each sending me back to revisit the page as I learned more of what was relevant.

My introduction to romance will be the subject of Chapter One: The Other Shoe, which will explain my ongoing passion for the genre among other things.

That introduction in 1996 would alter the intended course of my writing career as a science fiction / fantasy writer. It would lead me to write over fifty romance novels and a hundred short stories. Even the thrillers I've written have strong threads from that romance background. More importantly, it was the introduction to thinking about writing men in a whole new way.

The American Library Association's *Booklist* named three of my early romance novels "Top 10 Romance of the Year." Barnes & Noble named another as "Best 5

Romance of the Year" with NPR doing the same on yet another title. Night Owl Fiction, specializing in romance book reviews, granted me more than a dozen top star ratings and many "Top Pick of the Month" accolades.

I've studied and taught classes on many topics, but one of my favorites is the romance genre and how to bring those characters to life on the page, especially the male ones. This is my attempt to capture that passion in written form.

That's enough of that.

Introduction 1: Reality versus Fiction

Please consider this book as only the starting point, one guy's *guide,* planting trail markers along your journey to writing more engaging heroes. This is an attempt to explain the male experience in ways that will enhance your fictional men. In the writing process this also became my best effort at explaining the male experience. Any deeper understanding it provides of *real* men is purely coincidental but not accidental.

Our goal is to delve into *how* to remove fictional men from the clichéd world so many romance heroes appear to be trapped in. I'm not saying that the bad boy, the humble cowboy, the arrogant billionaire, etc. don't have their place. I do believe though that writers, and not only beginners, often fall into stereotypes without looking deeper.

It's by bringing the choices we make as writers into the conscious mind that we can improve our characters. It's too easy for our writing to fall into cliché and stereotype. This is a book about putting Prince Charming to the sword and helping your heroes pop on the page. No one benefits from stereotypes: not the writer, not the characters, not the real men in real life or the folks who love them.

But why do we want to go to all that extra work? And it *is* work. I love it deeply, but it isn't easy. (We're competing on an international stage called publishing. Did you expect it to be easy?)

If you're selling tens of thousands of copies (or more), why are you even reading this book? Seriously, if whatever you're doing seems to be working, don't clutter it up with my two cents.

Ah, but if you're not? Hopefully, this book will help you figure out why. The chances are very good that it's your hero's demise into cliché. We'll look at multiple ways to elevate the characters by going deeper into them, making them more visible, more lifelike. Will these tactics work on female characters as well? Absolutely, but they're not the primary focus here (though I will pay them occasional thought as we go).

Introduction 2: Writing Exercises

I'm a fan—and not—of writing exercises.
Write three sentences of a character in motion.
Write your character's view of this story from old age.
Write a ten-sentence scene about...

These mostly annoy the crap out of me. They did so as a beginner and they still do. But there is one that a teacher friend used that I absolutely love for newbie writer classes.

There's a wedding cake in the middle of an empty road. Why? Write ten sentences.

Then she'd have the students read them aloud. No two stories ever match—each is unique and different. Which is the point. That's the author's voice (we'll get to that). Then she'd read the short story *A Kind of Flying* from Ron Carlson's collection *Plan B for the Middle Class*, and discuss where the image came from. It was one of the stories we used at my own wedding. (Read it. Totally worth it.) Thanks, Ruth, for that one.

Past that level, I learned that the only style of writing exercise I like came from good friend and multi-bestselling author, Dean Wesley Smith: *The best exercise is the next book or story.*

In fact, he teaches that *every* moment at the keyboard is a learning experience. If you aren't learning, you aren't improving. And that's a nasty path to burnout for both you and your fans. I've seen it kill careers.

A tip? Exercise one thing at a time. If I've done my job, this book will give you a ton of ideas. If you try to do them all at once, your brain will lock up. It is one of the few paths to true writer's block.

Practice one new skill at a time—for the *entire* story or novel.

- *In this book I will practice male physicality.*
- *Ooo, a series of short stories, each practicing a different aspect of guy-speak.*

- *Next? Maybe I'll try using one to enhance the other.*
- *After that? Let me try the hero's journey. Then the augmented one after that.*
- And then...

Enough with the men, already. Go practice: setting, tension, pacing, family connections, dialogue, cliffhangers...then circle around and try guy-speak again. Now that earlier practice has had time to percolate into your deeper subconscious (aka your author voice—again, more on that later), your writing will start to shine in ways that three-sentence exercises would never achieve.

One further exercise here, and the motivation for doing it, is right in the title of this book, *One* Guy's Guide. These are my opinions and what I've learned by talking to and researching the men and women around me.

Go out and ask.

Ask friends, relatives, a spouse, invite all the boyfriends and husbands to your next romance book group and create a conversation. You'll be amazed at how willing people are to share and what you'll find out. I'd offer to Zoom into your group, but instead I wrote this book, so you're already holding my thoughts on writing men in romance.

Career Writing (side note)

If you're in this for the quick turn or as an amusing retirement project, more power to you.

If you're in this hoping to build a career as a writer,

you need to think longer term. I wanted to offer a quick side note so that it's in your thoughts as you consider what you'll read and hopefully learn as you continue through this book.

Tropes change.

They what? No, no. A bad boy with a heart of gold is a specific trope. That doesn't change. Does it?

Oh, but they do.

Here's one example: In the 1960s, the rape fantasy was a prominent romance trope. Hero rapes heroine, creating a sexual experience unlike any other, and they can't help but fall in love with each other. There's a trope that should never have been born in the first place and is now well dead and good riddance.

In the 1990s it had morphed into the "reluctant heroine" who merely needed to be pursued until she gave in, because "no" actually means "yes." He wears her down or proves it's true love. Nowadays we call that being a stalker. We're entering an age where, big surprise, no actually means no. Another one we're finally leaving in the dust.

In the early 2000s, I met a very distant relative who'd been a highly successful romance writer in the 1960s. She had finally recovered the publishing rights for all of her back list—and was taking down every one of the novels that she'd previously thought would bring income for life plus seventy years (the length of copyright). The problem? The rape fantasy trope went away, and she'd been one of the big names in that. We had a long discussion about what it would take to redraft those stories as more acceptable romances for a modern audience. I don't think she ever did.

Tropes change.

One of the many reasons this one changed? I suspect that at least in part it's that sexual assault numbers now are twenty percent of what they were in the 1960s, and that's despite the growing acceptance of reporting assault now capped by the MeToo culture. Even with how much it's in the news, the numbers have plummeted. A fantastic multi-generational trend.

And now that we're slicing and dicing generations more and more, we're seeing the tropes change faster than ever.

So, think about your bad boy, cowboy, billionaire, knight in shining armor... Think about the longer term. Even if you don't like rereading your own works (I *love* going back and revisiting my characters, every time I crack open an old title I lose hours), ask if you would be *comfortable* rereading it. Trust that instinct.

Are you writing about abuse and the horrid climb up to finding love again? Fine. Are you writing about abuse as a path to love? Well, that trope is dead. Think about what other assumptions you're making as you choose what to write about.

Here's a trope that died and sadly returned. In the espionage genre, the collapse of the Berlin Wall and the fall of the USSR killed the entire genre for most of twenty years. That change ended many, many careers. Am I saying they should have seen it coming? Probably not. Having lived through that time, it felt like it would last forever until we were all erased by a nuclear war. Sadly, it's back.

As you go through this book, and your own future writing, remember to keep checking in with yourself. Hint: the more you focus on enjoying what you write, the better off you're likely to be.

PART I

A BASIS TO BUILD FROM

1

THE OTHER SHOE

At the 1996 national conference of the Romance Writers of America, I fell flat on my face in front of an audience of eighty women and had an epiphany about sexism that launched me on a career of over fifty romance novels.

I sold my first novel to a terribly small romance house. By terribly small, I mean three-four novels per year…in a good year.

The editor wanted to prove that men could write romances—and to prove that her small press stood boldly on the cutting edge and deserved far more attention than, well, it actually deserved. So she took four male authors (two of us had sold her a book, the other two were students of hers) to a conference. Not just any conference, but RWA National in Dallas, Texas.

She arranged a spotlight session on the press. In front of a room of eighty women, she had the four of us and one female author each read a key structural scene from our novels.

A word about RWA Dallas in 1996. There were eighteen hundred women in attendance. There were a dozen presentations every hour. Talks by old pros with millions of books sold (literally), midlist authors on a particular topic of craft or business, and among those there was our tiny press.

These women attending the conference—from neophyte to the likes of Nora Roberts and Debbie Macomber—had one thing in common: they were all *incredibly* passionate about the business and writing of romance. Simultaneously daunting and inspiring, it was amazing as my first-ever writer's conference.

In all that week-long conference, there were seven male attendees who weren't on the business side, i.e. editors and agents. Yep, seven men were there as writers. It turned out that two of them weren't; they were boyfriends of attending female writers—being both supportive and bored out of their skulls. So actually five male writers: one writing successfully under a gender-neutral pen name and the four of us.

So, what happened?

We became absolutely and utterly invisible.

I had my first-sale sticker on my name badge, which is a big deal at that conference. Yet, if I asked a question during a session, it stopped the session as abruptly as if I'd thrown a wrench into a spinning gearbox. Then the qualification questions began:

- *You're a writer? (Not some boyfriend wasting our time.)*

- *You've written a novel? (Then not quite believing that...)*
- *You've sold a novel? (I'd hold up the First Sale banner on my badge.)*
- *Really? (Really!)*
- *Oh... (long pause) ...what was that question again?*

The same questions each time I spoke up (I considered having a t-shirt printed with the answers: *yes, yes, yes, & really*). I was a new writer, trying to figure out how to learn and how to elevate the notice of my writing by someone who could help advance my career in the writer's holy Mecca that was New York in that era. To that end, I worked very hard to come up with a good question in each session I attended. And, in turn, I received some wonderful answers...after the qualification round.

Curiously, I did make one important industry friend; one who in no way could reach down and affect the first faltering steps of my burgeoning career. She was one of the great powerhouses of romance publishing, come back from retirement for a single special project. She worked at such a strategic level that she didn't have anything to offer a flailing beginner. But I did love when, to everyone's surprise at future conferences, the great Carolyn Nichols always greeted me with a cry of pleasure and a big hug. She is sorely missed.

Anyway, back to RWA. Editors wouldn't speak to me in the hall because they assumed I was just wasting their time.

In roundtable sessions with agents, we each were allowed / expected to ask a question. When I asked mine, the (male) agent skipped over me and called on to the next person without answering. Even when one of the other attendees asked if he was going to answer my question.

Completely and utterly invisible.

When I returned to work the next week, I mentioned this experience to my female assistant. (And here's the crux of this whole section.)

Her response? "Well, duh!"

It took some explaining by her and several female friends. They all explained something that I don't have to describe for half of the world's population—women are sidelined, ignored, and seen as lesser-than because of their gender. Men's awareness of this?

In my youth, it was a not conscious phenomenon. "Pay gap" was the most the average man ever heard.

In the present day and age?

According to the 2023 World Economic Forum's "Global Gender Gap Report" (https://www3.weforum.org/docs/WEF_GGGR_2023.pdf), the US has risen about five percent against the global average in the last twenty years. Which barely bumps us into the top third of the hundred and forty-six nations assessed. For the geeks on this, they measure four areas and the index level is far more indicative than the actual rank. The US indexes within the top few percentage points for Educational Attainment (top 0.3% globally), and Health and Survival (top 3%). We're barely the top quarter for Economic Participation and Opportunity, and bottom quarter of the index for Political Empowerment. Sigh!

Well, we're getting there. At our current rate of

improvement, they estimate that the gender gap on those final two factors will be closed in only—a hundred and sixty years...or so. Personally, I'm banking on the new generations to kick ass.

Again, back to the conference.

For that week, the shoe was definitely on the other foot.

This was the moment that has shaped all my writing since. I'd received an abrupt education in what women had to do in our male-oriented society. I became utterly fascinated with the struggles women are forced to overcome and have focused on writing about powerful women ever since. And I've been told I do it well.

There was one distinct problem: I had no idea how to write *the men* they deserved. That I had to learn the hard way and is what I've attempted to capture in this book.

Back to that scene that I read to a room of eighty women, stunning them into silence. It was a blatant, graphic sex scene. One that I'd written as a ridiculous class exercise that the editor then insisted on shoehorning into my first novel. I immediately edited it back out once I recovered the rights.

The final twist? The novel that I sold to that small press that earned my first sale sticker at RWA National, and that I read the graphically salacious scene from (no wonder no New York editor would touch me)—was incongruously a light-hearted fantasy novel.

Oh, and though I'd go on to write over fifty of them, I actually *read* my first three romance novels—ever—at that conference, now almost thirty years in the past.

2

RESEARCHING: DARTAN'S STORY

THE MALE WRITERS IN MY CRITIQUE GROUP LAUGHED MY first attempt at a strong male character out of the room.

It was my second novel. (Thankfully long out of print and not worth finding one of the few copies that sold. Seriously. Not.) My first attempt at a science fiction romance, back before that was any kind of a thing, was not a glowing success.

Dartan, the antagonist / eventual protagonist, was *the* great warrior. He led the most lethal fighting force in the settled section of our arm of the Milky Way galaxy. I mean, this guy was tough and powerful and...

When I read his first scene, all the women in my critique group nodded and said he sounded like a good guy. And, yes, the men laughed at poor Dartan—loudly and derisively.

Being tenacious, week after week I revised that introductory scene, throwing it out, rebuilding it, throwing it away again. It was most of ten meetings before the men in the group conceded that, "Well, at least now he's a guy." Sadly, that's as high as poor Dartan ever climbed.

But he taught me that I was missing something. And clearly, I wasn't finding it in my beloved science fiction or in most of the romances I had begun inhaling. Or in all that many romances since.

So where to go to study men?

I'm not some extrovert, heading out to bars to hear the chatter. My main skill in sports is the effort I expend to not end up as a smear on the court when I foolishly tread upon one. My only two sports at all are volleyball and Frisbee; I threw a mean Ultimate Frisbee game in college (though I couldn't catch for crap). Neither of these is known for its macho guy-bonding camaraderic banter.

I started watching more thriller movies, but I need to throw up a caution flag here—a *huge* one! Movie writing is *not* book writing. If you wish to prove this to yourself, simply read scripts of a few of your favorite movies (The Internet Movie Script Database imsdb.com is a great resource for this.) Go ahead, read a Jason Bourne script. I dare you. He has fewer lines than just about any other major character in any movie. (In the fifth installment, *Jason Bourne,* he has twenty-five lines.)

Hint: neither is TV writing a good resource. If you write Joey from *Friends* without Matt LeBlanc as the actor bringing him to life, he's going to die as a cliché on the page.

So where to find that *authentic* male voice in the written form?

Autobiography is where I turned. Specifically, from the most *male* voices I could think of: Special Forces

Green Berets. Delta Force, SEALs, Night Stalkers, Marine snipers… There are now so many to choose from. Even with a ghost writer helping them out, it's as close as I could get to studying that deeply male voice.

Here are a few to get you started:

- *Warrior Soul* – Chuck Pfarrer
- *The Night Stalkers* and *In the Company of Heroes* – Michael J. Durant
- *Sully: My Search for What Really Matters* – Captain Chesley B. Sullenberger III (the pilot who landed the plane in the Hudson)
- *American Sniper* – Chris Kyle
- *No Easy Day* – Mark Owen (a lot of controversary over the facts, and that he broke a number of laws in writing it, but read for the voice)
- *Fight Like a Girl* – Kate Germano
- *Shoot Like a Girl* / *Fly Like a Girl* – Mary Jennings Hegar

I included a few for the women for a different view of the warrior's voice.

These next titles I offer with a word of caution: they're by journalists. Not putting down the reporting at all. Rather, it's that journalism by its very nature is a step back, a step removed. It's more about events, and the journalist's voice and feelings rather than the warrior's.

- *War* – Sebastian Junger
- *The Hurt Locker* – Mark Boal

- *Black Hawk Down* – Mark Bowden
- *Ashley's War* – Gayle Tzemach Lemmon

For a sailor, track down the fascinating *actual* journals of Christopher Columbus or Captain William S. Bligh. They differ widely from Nordhoff and Hall's fine tales of the *Mutiny on the Bounty* in form, content, and especially voice. They're old but rivetingly male voices.

Artic explorers, aviators, and Sherpa Tenzing Norgay's *Tiger of the Snows* of the conquest of Everest are out there waiting to be discovered. Even Anthony Bourdain's *Kitchen Confidential* and other writings.

Caution! This is one of those moments when you must be careful. I have read widely in real-life action adventure for much of a decade, and I still do when I find time. Almost none of these were written in the last ten or twenty years. If targeting a younger audience, think about the time frame of your hero, which leads to our next chapter.

If you need proof of this change across time, read Norgay's *Tiger of the Snows* followed by Jon Krakauer's *Into Thin Air,* written forty years apart. Read any Nora Roberts, then read Sarina Bowen. Or any Nicholas Sparks followed by John Green's *The Fault in Our Stars.*

Don't worry, I will be getting to all that I learned from this research. But ask yourself, what are *you* doing to learn more about writing convincing male characters?

3

TIME-FRAME-DRIVEN POINT OF VIEW

At the time of this writing, I'm a happily married, heterosexual male Baby Boomer in my mid-sixties. I was raised on folk music, Broadway shows, and MGM musicals, with my older sister bringing rock and roll into the house. And we were upper-middle class; Dad was a senior manager at IBM. Our family was also deeply dysfunctional without collapsing (quite) into utter chaos.

That is a very, very, *very* distinct point of view. I've worked hard to toss that aside as I've spent the last thirty years writing. And I look forward to doing the same for the next thirty. I don't want to be trapped in my own cliché any more than my heroes do.

I've done my best in this book to do the same or point out when I'm aware of that hereditarily nurtured point of view.

For yourself, you have to strive to understand your own perspective. What do you believe in? What do you bring to the page that's unique to you, your era, your upbringing? Be careful to ask yourself that constantly as you move through this book and when writing.

At my age, do I have the perspective to write an utterly engaging YA novel? Sure...if it's set in the 1960s or '70s. Set in the 2020s? Probably not. I could study, I *did* study. A few years ago, I read thirty or so award-winning YA novels, all published within the three prior years, to try to understand the younger audience better. (Tip: Go and ask your librarian for the most checked out YA romance novels...then put your name on the waiting list.)

My conclusion was that I should stick to what I know because WOW! were these authors ever writing in ways and about issues I could never replicate even when I could understand them. I'll bring this up in several places throughout this book.

Need proof? I got mine.

Once, when visiting my kid at college, she and her friends wanted to watch this great new sitcom together. *Freaks and Geeks,* set in 1980, was about the spunky misfits in high school that sent them all into fits of giggles. I actually had to leave the room because what to me had been traumatic experiences, to them were now powerless to hurt. I *love* that this had become a ridiculous comedy, though I still couldn't watch it without being physically ill.

I'm not saying that bullying doesn't exist or isn't brutal. I'm saying that it has changed in form and manner over time. (And I'm hoping there's less of it overall, but I don't know.)

Be aware of this in your writing.

Be conscious that your point-of-view of the male romance hero may have no relation to mine as you read this. The tools should still work, but the voice, *your* voice, may track along a whole different highway.

4

THE AUTHOR'S VOICE

I hadn't planned on including this chapter, but it keeps coming up, so I'll spend a few moments with this topic. (And yes, someday I expect I'll write a book about Author Voice that's in my head.) I just reread that sentence and now I'm laughing. No, someday I will *not* write a nonfiction book about *the voices in my head*—that's how I make my living in fiction.

Author voice is what happens when you get out of your own way.

Seriously, that's the core of it.

Will you recognize it or hear it? Probably not. Why? Because, if you're hitting it, it sounds like you on the page.

But how do you find it?

Write a lot, edit a little.

The more you write, the more comfortable and automatic the craft of writing becomes. When you slip into storytelling mode—without considering sentence structure, repeated words, how to handle a character's growth arc—is when you start approaching voice.

Again, it's you!

For me, it is much like my conversational tone. Smart, a little wry humor, reveling in building tension, playing with both the words and the characters, and always a deeply romantic subtheme with an underlying sympathy (probably all those MGM musicals my mom so loved when I was a kid).

It is also woman-forward. It doesn't matter if it's romance, thriller, or science fiction; every title I write is strongly woman-forward. I write the men they deserve, whether in a romance or simply in the adventure, but that's not at the heart of my writer's voice.

Do I think about all that as I write? Hell no!

So how did I find it? Curiously, by *not* going out looking for it. Instead, I sought to avoid artifice, cliché, imitation of other authors, and especially overthinking. When I'm writing, I just write. (Caveat, I think *a lot* about story when I'm writing, but not *how* I'm writing it.) When I edit, I try to do it as lightly as possible.

A brief reprise to Dartan's story above, and the novel that followed. Both were edited to death. The former by the editor of that small press and the latter by me using the techniques that editor had instilled in my head as *required*. Both books were edited until there wasn't a hint of the author's voice left in either manuscript. Yep, they both became absolutely, soullessly flat.

Think back to that writing exercise of the wedding cake in the middle of the road. Whatever story you wrapped around that image is a strong indicator of your author voice: dark, funny, tragic, where they'd buried the dead body of the rich but nasty relative just before the road was paved... Yep! That. What are your romances like: sweet, bad boy, billionaire dreams, powerful women, meek women, meek men, YA, suspense-ridden, goth... Yep! That.

So, how do you find out what your author's voice is? You keep writing. The more natural it feels, the closer you get. If you decide you need to know, consider asking your growing fan base to offer you a few words that they use to describe your writing to a friend.

I did something a little different.

I had someone toss all of my reviews into a Word document. From Amazon, B&N, Goodreads, the traditional reviewers who wrote up my books, and so on. Don't *read* the reviews. The bad ones can be devastating and the great ones can be very hard to get past.

I had a stumper of a review from my second editor about a new manuscript I'd submitted (#5 in a series), "This is the best book you've ever written. When do I get the next one?" The next one was a blank white page at that time. How in the world was I supposed to write something / anything after that review? I eventually did, but those first chapters were a hard slog because of a *great* review. Just don't read them.

Anyway, I took all of those reviews that my assistant (my ever-patient wife) had gathered, and tossed them into a word cloud generator. Yes, the reviews were rife with all the romance words: passion, romance, hero, heroine, love... But they also had a heavy preponderance of thriller keywords: tension, action, thrilling, edge-of-seat, couldn't put down...

It was this exercise that told me perhaps—*perhaps*—

my natural voice lay more to the thriller side than the romance side. Looking back five years later, I can see that each of my most popular romance books leaned heavily toward romantic thriller. So much so that almost all my fans followed me for the transition to pure thrillers.

The other aspect I've observed is that voice evolves. We authors are no more static than our characters. We grow and change in interesting and curious ways. As we do, our voice shifts with us. Probably so subtly that we'll never notice...because, if we do it right, it matches the voice inside our heads.

5

FALLACIES

He answered her opening her heart to him with a grunt. Had he even heard her? How could she tell?

The answer to her question arrived moments later. He grasped the tattered remnants of her blouse in one mighty fist and tore them aside with a gesture so powerful it echoed all the way down to her loins.

After wrenching aside her lace panties, he took her in one orgasmic blast she would never recover from.

As he emptied himself into her, and she dug her nails into his back that would mark him long past the wounds' healing, he knew this was what true love felt like.

Okay, it's over-the-top ridiculous...except that I've read only slightly expanded versions of this scene far too many times.

There are three distinct fallacies in this one little example: The Continuum Fallacy, The Consistency

Fallacy, The True-to-cliché versus True-to-self Fallacy. So, let's dive in and do a little exploring.

The Continuum Fallacy

I'll never understand why this one is so overlooked. This is going to sound insanely simplistic, and yet how many stories have you read where the man is the embodiment of the characteristics at the far left of the list below:

- Silent Effusive
- Grunts Erudite
- Strong Weak
- Tall Short
- Powerful Total Lame-o
- Always action first Thinks before acts
- Emotionless (even robotic) Feeling
- Utterly self-confident Rife with self-doubt

No one, not even a cliché, is all the way at one extreme.

Are you going to write a silent, powerful warrior who only speaks in grunts—and keeps us riveted for three hundred and fifty pages? If so, you're a better writer than I am.

On top of that, nobody exists in one state all the time. The grunting man will never profess his love in poetic terms. But he may struggle to do so and his attempts will not be his most confident moments. There's a lovely speech on precisely this point by Kenneth Branagh in the movie *Much Ado About Nothing*. Smitten by love, he attempts to commit poetry...and utterly fails. Being Branagh, he also does it with great humor.

Think about these various states and play with them. Imagine a man who is never confident or powerful, except around the one right woman. If you can figure out how to write him, he'll exist on the page. An unlikely example?

Consider Neo in *The Matrix,* who only finds his confidence when he's around Trinity. In the whole opening half hour of the movie (or longer), he's utterly hopeless. And almost every time she's out of range, he utterly dissolves into some lower state of being.

However, it isn't the overworked reverse trope of powerful woman saves weak man. It's rather that he becomes his better / best self in her presence. He's lifted up. This is a core tool I use as I love doing gender role reversal.

Actually, the more I think about it, the less I think that's what it is. I typically flip only one of the gender's roles—removing the woman from the subservient lesser-than role.

The Consistency Fallacy

This is an incredibly dangerous fallacy because, when it's broken, it breaks the reader's connection to the character. Look back at my ridiculous hero. He grunts, he beds her wildly, he is *not* going to then consider that this is what true love feels like. He might thank her. Probably for her willingness when he needed a woman the way he needed her. Or perhaps he'll think that there'd never been a woman like her that he couldn't control himself around. But true love? No, no, and, did I mention, no.

Now take a gentle hero, one who is not out to conquer the world—not even if it turns out that's what he must do. He *might* think about how much he loves this woman, or how he could never find another like her.

The bad boy with the heart of gold isn't going to stop acting like the bad boy, simply because he's doing the right thing. The likelihood of the cowboy waxing poetic about the glories of the bluebonnet flowers dotting the Texas prairie strikes me as equally unlikely. And I've read both far too many times.

A character can grow—they'd better grow or why are you writing about them—but except in odd corners like redemption romance, they will not change who they are to a degree where the character is inconsistent.

The True-to-cliché versus True-to-self Fallacy

This one give me nightmares.

The same day I started this section, I was speaking at a conference about secondary characters. Here's a paraphrase of one of my points that the panel absolutely agreed on.

"In school we were taught that there was something called a quarter-round character. There's the main character, their primary friends, antagonists, and so forth. But if you have a minor walk-on character, they don't need to be fully fleshed out."

I argued that this was an absolute fallacy. If a character appears on the page at all, they must have purpose. Like a movie, the *extras* are off in the background. If they arrive center screen—speaking, acting, interacting with the story that in any way affects the plot or the other characters—they *can't* be a cliché. They must be themselves.

And once a character is their so-to-speak own person, they won't—they *can't*—exist in the land of cliché.

Are there clichéd characters in my books? More than I would care to admit to. But this is something I fight back against with all the power I can.

Is the bad boy a cliché? A particularly annoying one. Why? Because he's another lascivious, clueless male stereotype.

Fine, how do you fight back against that?

Ask the *Five Whys*. I didn't think this up; it is a common tool in the corporate environment for drilling down to the core information. These aren't five separate questions; these are a sequence to peel aside the layers and discover the root cause behind the character.

1. Why is he a bad boy? Because he's rebelling against his immigrant parents.
2. Why is he rebelling against them? Cliché might suggest that they abused him or ignored him, but what if they were model citizens running a successful restaurant? Perhaps it's because he feels that he could never live up to their standards of success.
3. Why does he feel that he could never meet their standards? Because he thinks of the challenges they met to come to Washington,

DC, and cook true to themselves and their heritage. This, in turn, sets an example that his easy life of growing up in such a household is something he could never live up to.

4. Why does he feel he can't live up to that? Because he's already in this country. He's never going to start a two-star Michelin restaurant on his own. He knows that nothing he does can ever be up to that standard.
5. Why does he feel he can never live up to their standard? Because he loves them so much that his worst nightmare is disappointing them. And in utterly losing his way, that's exactly what he does.

These are the questions that created Wild Tim Maloney in my *Take Over at Midnight,* The Night Stalkers #4. Did I ask these as I created the character? Only a little. But while writing him, I kept tossing out the obvious answers until I essentially had asked the five whys.

By avoiding cliché, by digging down deeper into the character, my bad boy becomes more real, more engaging, and made my readers more likely to keep reading.

But that isn't where I stopped fleshing out that character.

Tim is a joker at heart. For example, when his military action team is called away on a secret mission, an Army Ranger (the "quarter-round character") overhears there's an upcoming assignment and wants in on the action. He can't go, because he doesn't have the security clearance, and I could leave it there. It tells the reader that the mission is more exciting and more dangerous than any amount of description could do.

However, Tim does *not* leave it there. He tells the guy that they're flying out of the remote hot desert base to pick up twenty gallons of ice cream that a colonel sent their way. "Get everyone together, because it'll already be melting by the time we get it back here."

As he flies off on the mission, the heroine asks, "What the hell?"

He leaves it to her to figure out, which she does because they're soulmates who don't know it yet.

"Oh." Lola got it. They'd have tables and bowls and spoons all set out and lined up within minutes of the helicopter's taking off. And then a couple dozen Rangers and about fifty base and SOAR personnel would wait.

And wait.

When the ice cream never showed up, everyone would pound on the poor, dumb Ranger who'd bought Tim's line. With one sentence he'd stirred up several days' worth of entertainment.

Suddenly we can picture this poor, formerly-quarter-round soldier, standing there with his spoon at the ready in the desert camp, with a whole line of his teammates about to beat the crap out of him. He's no longer just a cliché gung-ho trooper. In two or three lines, he gains a personality, depth...and an uncertain future.

Another Example

Let's take a pair of characters from another of my novels just to discuss other aspects of this. It doesn't matter whether or not you've read the book, I'm just using them because it's easier than using some other title you may or may not have read. This is about Archie and Kee from *I Own the Dawn,* Night Stalkers #2.

Place on Continuum
>Archie: Quiet, patient, thoughtful, educated
>Kee: Warrior, impatient, action-focused, streetwise

Consistency

Archie: Wealthy upper-crust Boston, boarding schools, no best friend as such, West Point grad, concludes hard work always triumphs. He has been a top copilot for five years (rather than vying for a command of his own), not close to his parents, he adopts a war orphan they rescue together, and he's gone on Kee from the first moment (in classic romance *heroine* style).

Kee: East LA street kid, grew up as a gang member, GED, best friend gunned down in a drive-by, concludes she must fight for everything. She's a top warrior (but her units eventually crumble around her because she's kinda impossible), has no parents, does her best to shed the war orphan into a refugee camp or child services, thinks her only weapons are her gun and her body.

If True-to-cliché

Archie: convinces Kee that love is real, he (being the guy) saves the day.

Kee: does her final act for the sake of that love.

True-to-self

Archie: gives up on her as being impossible.

Kee: saves the day, and her final act as a sniper teaches her the pain and power of true love.

Yes, there's some gender swapping going on here. But consider a few points:

- Neither character is at the extreme of any continuum. They are a mix of characteristics.
- Even in this vastly oversimplistic explanation of these characters, they are internally consistent over time.
- And that consistency includes being true-to-self.
- When they show up in later books, you can still see their absolute consistency, little mellowed by their years together.

Blurring Lines

The lines between the sexes and genders are blurring fast, and faster every day.

A whispered, "He might be gay" didn't even exist in my high school. Now LGBTQ+ has parades and lands daily in the news (sometimes even for the right reasons) with rainbow flags flying.

A male-female dichotomy can now be scoffed at as "so old-fashioned." It warms my heart because I've always had this outrageous theory that people are, well, people.

Keep blurring those lines! Please.

PART II
GUY-SPEAK

6

THE KISS

THIS CHAPTER IS ABOUT A BRIEF BUT ILLUSTRATIVE SCENE from the sitcom *Friends*, Season 2 Episode 7. Two characters, Ross and Rachel, have just really kissed for the first time. Here's a link to the one-minute-long scene that is available at the time of this writing.

https://www.youtube.com/watch?v=23-hBKl86Y4

(If the link is no longer valid, try searching on "Friends Rachel Tells About the Kiss.")

Or just read on.

Here's the gist of the scene:

Rachel faces her two women friends after sharing that Ross kissed her. They effuse and want details. Along with silenced phones and glasses of wine, there's excitement, discussion of the kiss, hand positions, implications, and ultimately happy sighs of how romantic it was.

Cut to the three guys sharing a pizza while standing around a foosball game table.

> *Ross:* And then I kissed her.
> *Joey:* Tongue?
> *Ross:* Yeah.
> *Joey:* Cool.
> *Chandler nods his agreement.*
> *Meaning:* It was a good kiss. *Easy sitcom laugh.*

But what if we were to dig a little deeper? (As I exercise the audacity to second guess the writers of one of the most successful shows in recent television history.)

> *Joey:* Tongue?
> *Ross:* Yeah.
> *Joey (hesitates and looks thoughtful):* Cool.
> *Meaning:* it was her choice, so it's okay. *This is Joey the friend of Ross but also the friend of Rachel.*

But this is still low-hanging fruit. It's still an obvious line. Cute, funny, a little depth, but what if we play with it some more to get more character depth and richness?

> *Joey:* Tongue?
> *Ross (hesitates):* Yeah. *(almost a question as he studies Joey carefully)*
> *Joey (considers):* Cool. *(It was her choice.)*
> *Ross:* Look of relief. *(So, Joey isn't going to beat the crap out of me.)*
> *Meaning:* Joey the Protector emerges, *a role*

he embraces more and more in later seasons.

Personally, I think this version is the most typical guy-speak. There's a lot going on in this version that we'll dissect in a moment, but I want to offer a few other ways this might have gone.

- *Joey the Capital-M Man:* He grabs Ross by the shirt, pushes him up against the refrigerator, and demands, "You ask her first?"
- *Joey the Capital-M Man Uber-Protector:* He grabs Ross by the throat, slams him up against the refrigerator, and demands, "You touched one of the girls?"
- *Joey the Crass:* "Did you do the dirty? Right there in Central Perk? Which chair? Or was it on the couch? Had to be the couch! Next time for coffee, I got dibs on the couch!"
- *Joey the...*

You get the idea.

Subtext

The women speak mainly in words.

Much of guy-speak is in the subtext.

Look at the first three versions above. There are only three words spoken in each one, the exact same words: *Tongue, Yeah, Cool.* Yet the meanings shift: easy laugh, the good friend, the defender.

This is a very common and generally real version of how guys communicate. We already know what the parts of the conversation are, especially among friends, and the dialogue is built on top of that.

Silence has meaning. Implied understand has meaning.

This conversation between the three women and the three guys occurs very early in a series that ultimately ran for a decade. As I mentioned, had this same conversation happened later, I expect we would have gotten a version closer to my third version and that the laugh would have been different—less comic, more "Yeah, Joey would pound Ross but good if he stepped out of line with Rachel."

Again, it's a sitcom by very successful writers. I'm simply suggesting that for your characters to come to life on the page, where Matt LeBlanc isn't hanging out on your page making the most of it for the readers, we need to dive deeper and spell it out more clearly to create richer characters and therefore greater reader engagement.

Low-Hanging Fruit

This is a phrase I used earlier that I think bears some clarification before we move on.

Low-hanging fruit in story terms is the easy idea, the low fruit that's easiest to pick. However, the sweetest fruit is typically high up on the tree, exposed to the sun.

The same is true in storytelling.

The first idea is easy. The next idea isn't much harder. By the third or fourth idea, now you're getting interesting.

Think back to Kee. She's the tough gunner, not Archie. She's the one who acts like the warrior. And she's the one most disconnected from her emotions. In fact, she's so disconnected that when they finally escape from her control, they blast forth in ways that essentially destroy her relationship with the hero. (They eventually rebuild them because this is a romance after all.)

Bypassing the low-hanging fruit is an essential step to avoiding the clichéd male character. Cliché, by its very nature, is the lowest hanging fruit of all.

Emotions

As a side note, I sometimes get the question: do guys even feel emotions?

Oh yeah, we do. We may not want to talk about them. We may not have the words or practice of talking about them, but we absolutely have emotions.

What this means is that they will crop up in the most unexpected ways at odd times and places. We'll get into some examples of this below.

7

EXTREME GUY-SPEAK

FIRST, A CAVEAT. NOTE THE WORD IN THIS CHAPTER'S title: Extreme. A millennial, I'm assured, would never speak this way. Men of my generation definitely would. The cross-over happened somewhere in between. Think about that carefully in writing your men.

Let's take a look at high-level commanders. I've met a number of guys who are team leaders, even ship captains: an oil tanker, a submarine, and a destroyer among others. And one of the things that most of them share is the real-world cliché of having one face.

This is the composite-him: happy, angry, afraid, sad, and weeping inside.

Inside is the key, he processes everything internally. When something is really troubling him, he goes even more silent than usual. But once he's gotten through it, he's back to his normal, albeit quiet self.

So, let's build a story about him as an example of extreme guy-speak.

Making Up Story

Let's say his wife leaves him.

Maybe they were into sports and had season tickets to some team (or plays, symphony, opera…). Over the years, season ticket holders get to know the other season ticket holders seated around them.

One day, the wife is no longer there. Word gets around through the wives' network that she left him. This filters to the husbands, who probably buy him an extra beer a couple times, without any particular explanation of why—guy-speak sympathy.

He doesn't acknowledge it, perhaps beyond a slight raising of his cup in a toast before the first sip. To do more would bring the reason too close to the surface. Not comfortable.

Does he turn in the seat?

No, she might come back.

She marries someone else; he still keeps the seat.

It sits there empty, game after game for a season, maybe two or three. If she ever wanted to come back, he's saying the door is open. Not that he'd ever say to her face how much he cared about her. His presence for the years before should make that clear.

One day, he meets a new woman. After a while, he decides that he likes her enough to bring her to the game.

What happens when she sits in that seat?

He doesn't say a word. Not to anyone. He says, "This is Jen," then watches the game.

When he goes to the restroom during the seventh inning stretch, a couple guys go with him. "Where did you two meet?" As if that's the important question. It actually is, because they know it had to be major for him to invite her to sit in the ex-wife's seat. No need to hash that out. And that they choose that question means also that they like her and are offering tacit approval. If they didn't, they might choose a tease of, "She doesn't know crap about baseball." Or maybe, "Good to see you trying on *someone* for size again."

Back at the seat, the women are left to—perhaps resentfully but perhaps not because he *is* a good guy—lift the emotional cargo for him. They do this by explaining how our silent guy has sat next to an empty seat for three years since his wife left him.

So, Jen gets the information—in words—that he thinks she's really, really special. He never had to say a word of that to her, the other women did it for him (if one is younger, she's sure to smack him on the back of the head, without explaining herself, when he returns). And, by the way, even on their wedding day, he probably never will say it. He'll say, "I do," which should be clear enough, right? (Deep, old-fashioned, guy-speak.)

He feels the emotion but doesn't feel *the need* to say a word to communicate it.

And yes, this is probably an accurate account of how his story would go if any of these friends were to land in the middle of it in real life. This kind of modern, younger male? He'll never get a second date—ever.

The reason I spelled this out so thoroughly is to show that to a man, of any generation, silence has power. Timing and expression of emotion don't have to be external—especially not for a guy.

Actions Speak Louder

In our silent guy's favor, or any romantic hero's, is that his actions will often speak louder than he can. Our über-silent hero brought her to the game. He made sure that she had beer, peanuts, whatever she wanted. A hat hawker will come up the aisle and he'll glance at her, then nod toward the hawker to ask if she wants one. This guy is guaranteed to open doors, hold the tickets, and carry the bags.

He isn't questioning the woman's ability (unless he's a misogynistic jerk), he's extending every courtesy he knows to tell her that he cares about her.

I do most of the driving in our one-car household. Not because I think my wife isn't a good driver, she's better than I am. But she hates the incredibly narrow streets where we now live and the busy highways if we're going farther away. I drive to spare her those. The moment we're out on the blue highways or country roads, we're both safer if I let her take over.

Cultures

This also happens across cultures. There are cultures in which showing any negative emotion is treated as very narcissistic. A cross-cultural marriage of a Western-level emoting woman and a culturally emotion-abhorring man...

Why? The man has been trained he must be strong. Or perhaps the whole culture teaches that you must never be weak or you're dragging down the whole community.

You get the idea. It may work, but it will never be easy. Which could make for some great fiction.

8

SOME EXAMPLES

Two Women in Guy-Speak

LET'S START BACK WITH OUR POOR STREET FIGHTER TURNED military warrior, Kee Smith. I mentioned before that teams always seem to break down around her—however, she's never met a commander like Major Emily Beale. I'm using women characters here, but I very specifically had them use only guy-speak with each other.

This is the first half of a warrior military-speak conversation. They're discussing far more than the war orphan girl Kee rescued earlier in the book and has been unable to place in a refugee camp or with some military form of child services:

"Major, I wanted to say—"

"Are you quitting on me, Smith?" Major Emily Beale's voice was sharp over the open intercom. Any possibility of humor nowhere on the radar.

"Night Stalkers Don't Quit," Kee replied without

thinking. That's one of the reasons she'd wanted to join in the first place. NSDQ was more than the Night Stalkers motto, it was their first rule of life. SOAR fliers *never* quit. *She* never quit.

Beale swiveled until she was staring back at Kee between the two pilot seats. In the dim instrument glow of the night-flight cabin, Kee could see Beale's face. A way she hadn't seen it before. Not pretty, nor with that rare open smile that lit her up. Her face was the dead serious of a seasoned SOAR flight commander.

"You quitting on that girl?"

Kee gritted her teeth and glared back at Beale, eye to eye.

"Night Stalkers Don't Quit!"

"Right. Until you do, we don't have a problem." She turned back to the flight controls.

Then a hundred pages later, Kee is covered in dried blood that she's cleaned out of the helicopter she flies in. She was absent from a mission, in order to take care of the war orphan, and her replacement was horribly shot up:

Emily moved to stand before the Sergeant.

Kee slowly raised her head until she looked at Emily.

Her eyes were dark hollows, her normally sun-kissed complexion gray with exhaustion.

"Are you quitting on me, Smith?"

Kee blinked once, slowly, as if waking from a dream. "Night. Stalkers. Don't. Quit." She ground it out from a throat raspy with lack of use. But the eyes had fire in them. Whatever drove Kee Smith still shone brightly.

Emily didn't know at what moment she made her decision, but she completed the ritual.

"Right. Until you do, we don't have a problem."

She turned and walked away, unable to face the pain in the young woman's eyes.

Go back and look at the dialogue in both these passages. We know exactly what they're talking about, even when it's multiple things. But the deliberate use of guy-speak simplifies it. Now imagine the same conversation between Clint Eastwood or Chris Pratt and some raw recruit. It absolutely still works.

Two Guys in Guy-Speak

Let's try another, between two guys this time. PriFly is the control tower on an aircraft carrier, high on the superstructure and surrounded by glass. They're standing on the narrow outside walkway used for cleaning the glass. They're discussing then-Captain Emily Beale getting shipped stateside on no notice.

Mark leaned his forearms on the PriFly's rail so that they both stared aft at the glittering sea.

"Something's got you on this one."

"I'm worried because she's my best pilot." Sounded plausible enough.

"She?" Jim shot an elbow at his ribs and Mark barely blocked it.

"Eat hot lead!"

"Ooo! Touchy, touchy!" Jim started laughing, then chopped it off. "One of yours? She? Tell me you're not going there, Mark."

"I'm not going there." Only one kiss worth. And all that had earned him was a wrenched arm and a Coke shower.

"Don't go there. You know that." Jim looked around and then leaned in close. "And don't be telling me this. I can't know this. Stick around. I'll hook you up with a cute midshipman. At least she'll be in another service. Please tell me she's not part of your squad."

Mark did his best to look bland but knew it didn't work.

Jim let out a low whistle.

"You got it bad?"

Mark shrugged.

"Aw, shit!"

Take especial note of that final sequence.

Jim let out a low whistle.

"You got it bad?"

Mark shrugged.

"Aw, shit!"

His buddy Jim knows that if a commander with the integrity of company commander Major Mark Henderson has crossed the line in any way of even considering fraternization with a woman in the chain of his command, that he's either in love or really close. From that Jim knows that there's no changing the situation, no matter how much trouble it's going to cause. All he can do then? Offer his sympathy, "Aw, shit!"

Man and Woman in Guy-Speak

One final example. Emily Beale gets shipped to the White House. She gets surprised by the head of the Presidential Protection Detail inside the Residence—and flattens his ass. Later in the story, he comes to take her to the West Wing for a meeting, after she runs to change her clothes. This is guy-speak between genders.

> "I'll meet you in three minutes where I dropped you like a brick." A part of her simply couldn't resist poking the beast.
> He favored her with a nearly feral smile. "You are welcome in the Secret Service sparring gym any time you want." If smiles could kill.
> They laughed together.
> Briefly.
> Chopped off in unison.
> Maybe she'd now made an enemy into a friend. A dangerous one, but a friend.

Each time, a whole conversation occurs that isn't necessarily in the speech or even the topic of guy-speak. It's not a secret code, but it's one that most of those who speak it understand well.

9

THE "VOICE"

I'VE HEARD IT CALLED MANY THINGS: THE DEFINITIVE Voice, The Didactic Voice, Like He's Speaking God's Own Truth. Again, this is a fading reality, thank God.

It was ubiquitous in my generation, and I've heard it occasionally in the Millennials, but it's far rarer.

Most women, regrettably, know this one all too well. If you're a guy, and very observant, watch the women in the audience the next time some lecturer slips into that voice. The eye rolls will reign rampant around the room. Subtly, because women, of my generation at least, are trained to never show disapproval of a man to that man.

I've watched younger women ignore that rule with amazement and joy.

My father used this tone constantly to confirm his power, even when I could prove he was flat-out wrong. As a way of confirming authority, it's taught to men of my generation (sorry to keep throwing in this caveat, I'll try to cut down, but it means that my generation taught it to their sons who may have taught it to...).

It serves many purposes for men, consciously or not. We're taught by our fathers, the military, the police, the medical establishment, and many others that it is the best way to portray confidence. And that confidence is how to lead.

Perhaps that's one of the big problems with getting women into leadership roles. Men protecting their turf, against women who are deeply trained to include appeasing caveats and qualifiers into their speech patterns that utterly fail the test of male-style confident communication. Hmmm... It sure isn't ability holding them back.

The Fading Voice

I've asked a few Millennials and one wasn't even sure what I'm referring to. Yay! Progress.

Discovering "The Voice"

I thankfully had someone smack this voice out of me, mostly, at seventeen. I ran the high school theater for most of two years. The two classes before had graduated. The class ahead of me had no one who'd been taught to lead. Then, senior year, the school didn't give the *great* drama teacher tenure and he left. I ended up being the one to step into the vacuum.

With a horrid (to put it kindly) *new* drama teacher, the entire play landed on the shoulders of myself and a fellow theater nut. And we gave it our all to bring the show to life. She worked with actors, makeup, and costumes (she was a way better director and really good with people); I focused on schedules, set building, and lighting.

It was a big show, with a fair-sized cast and a large crew to build the massive set I'd designed—many of them new to the theater. The stress showed as I tried to be everywhere at once, often shouting across the theater rather than running over to answer a question, then running back to whatever I was doing.

One day a freshman girl from the makeup crew came up to me in the midst of everything and said, "You know, you scare me to death." Then she walked away. After standing in stunned silence for a couple minutes, I walked back to the room where they were practicing makeup (all prior knowledge had graduated or not been tenured, so the crew were experimenting on each other to learn).

I sat down and, quietly, asked why.

That's when I learned that I'd been speaking as if I wielded God's Own Voice. I immediately began shedding it.

Insidious Depth of "The Voice"

And to give you an idea of how deeply ingrained it is in the male psyche, two decades later, when I finally found the right woman and had the good fortune to marry her, she called me on it again.

"But I don't do that!"

Turns out I did, but I did it differently. I would speak a declarative sentence in The Voice and then mentally step aside and see if it made sense—which it often didn't. But I wasn't doing that last step out loud. So, at first, I made that extra step out loud because I couldn't stop that tone all at once. Declaration! "Huh, nope, that doesn't sound right. So what is?"

I just checked in with my wife while writing this and she said I don't do even that anymore. Whew!

Being conscious of or actually shedding The Voice is *very* unusual for a man, especially of my generation. Or the generation we trained. How about in the generation you're writing?

That's why I wrote all this. To bring it conscious in your writing. Play with this. Is the didactic tone something your hero uses? Ask the five whys. Self-defense? Or perhaps your villain uses it because it makes him sound more evil?

It *is* reality, but use it as a tool and it adds another layer of realism and depth.

10

A FEW FINAL GUY-SPEAK THOUGHTS

REMEMBER, IT'S ALL A CONTINUUM. THERE ARE VERY FEW guys actually as cryptic as my composite commander-friend above when it comes to real life.

Example 1

In The Night Stalkers #6, *By Break of Day*, I have the romance of Michael Gibson. Introduced in Book #1, he lurked along in the background of all the books in between. Michael is that super warrior that poor Dartan of earlier could never achieve. He's the best fighter in Delta Force, which probably makes him the best in the world.

Delta Force—unlike the overly chatty SEAL Team 6 (technically called DEVGRU)—are known as the ones who never talk. So, for five books, Colonel Michael Gibson almost never speaks and certainly not about anything as fuzzy as an emotion.

In his book, I do *not* have the cruelty to pair him with

a voluble, chatty love interest who wants him to show his heart. Instead, Captain Claudia Jean Casperson is almost as quiet as he is, though she absolutely understands emotions.

This book has alarmingly little dialogue. My editor wanted me to unwrap Michael, show his softer, emotional side. It's not who he is. I'm no longer with that house, but when I run into her at the occasional conference, she still asks me, "Does that book actually sell with no dialogue?" Yes, it does, very nicely.

Why? Because his past and his present are internally and externally consistent, even during the complex process of falling in love.

Example 2

If you wish to study men who know how to talk, I'm going to break my own rule about avoiding television show writing, and point you toward a television series. Watch either the original series of *Queer Eye for the Straight Guy* or the new *Queer Eye*.

Some of those men are pretty quiet, but some are so chatty you wonder why they don't go hoarse on every show. They make a fascinating study of the spectrum from reserved to voluble, all within a single cast.

Example 3

In my Where Dreams contemporary romance series, one of the heroes is an Italian chef. Everything is big and boisterous. He is past-consistent, which includes being very chatty. It fits the character that he wears his heart on his sleeve. When he falls for an Alaskan lawyer who has made it a careful study to be unexpressive—and perhaps even unaware—of her own feelings, that becomes but one of the many problems he'll face as a romantic hero.

A Backward Example

As a reminder that we're all on a continuum…

I'm genetically a hundred percent Jewish and my wife is half Scottish, leaning heavily to that side from her pure-blood Scottish single mom. The Scots have a very stoic, can-do attitude; we Jews have a very long history of kvetching. Think of Tevye in *Fiddler on the Roof* looking up at the heavens and saying to God, "I know we are the chosen people, but once in a while, can't you chose someone else?"

My wife *always* knows what I'm feeling. So much so that she's developed an in-house phrase when I'm being excessively expressive: *Turn it down to stun.*

Her Scottish side? I've learned that when she's upset, my best move is *not* to follow my instincts to step forward and nurture and discuss. Instead, it works best if I go away and leave her in silence to do that internal processing thing I mentioned above.

Yes, your fictional male hero might well work either way. Now start asking about how to increase the pressure on him—more tension typically means a more engaging story.

- The heroine can't stop pushing him to speak: She either gets a dose of possibly too much information, can expect a blow up, or a total retreat from the silent man.
- The man's friend drops in for a visit: One friend will get him aside and talk. A different one may get him aside but not say a word, or will chat with the heroine allowing the hero to brood/process off to the side.
- The girl's friend drops in for a visit: The talkative guy may either land in the middle of a three-way conversation where he blurts everything out (perhaps wholly embarrassing the heroine in front of her friend), or he may flounder about helplessly at the interrupted conversation. The silent processing man may or may not stage a retreat, but he'll welcome the chance to keep his thoughts to himself.
- The external plot crisis escalates and requires action: both your expressive and non-expressive man will probably tuck away his feelings—for now—and deal with it. The more emotional male may come right back to it, or even lace it in throughout the crisis. The less expressive one may be completely done processing it, without saying a word, while dealing with the crisis.

These are but a few variations.

11

ANOTHER FINAL GUY-SPEAK THOUGHT

We are all the results of our upbringing as I mentioned in the introduction. For a man in Western culture, perhaps even more so in Eastern culture, this plays out in so many ways.

For example, we're taught that we must be strong. It's up to the guy to take care of the woman, the family, the career...blah, blah, blah. And if we're failing at any of these, it only makes it ten times worse on our egos. Suddenly we're failing at the primary way we've been trained is our measure of strength.

This same effect holds true for the man that we write about.

In order to appear powerful, he can't be going around riddled with self-doubt.

Actually, that's not quite accurate. He can't be going around *appearing* to be riddled with self-doubt. Because all except the most arrogant and most oblivious men are. That fact typically won't show until you're a very close friend. And the two of you are alone. And the mood just happens to be right. And...

Yeah, guys are trained not to show self-doubt; they may not even be aware they're having any. If you want a tiny example that they do, watch a guy's hands, especially in a new situation or when meeting someone they're attracted to. If their hands are always shifting from pockets (too casual) to clasped (oops, that looks like I'm holding my crotch) to crossed arms (no, someone told me that's negative despite it being a comfortable position) to leaning an elbow on the bar to... It's because he has self-doubt about what to do with his hands. He's, consciously or not, trying to appear somehow normal, interested, attractive, in control, or whatever.

The doubts exist.

Also, there's a point made earlier that needs to be emphasized. Think back over the guy-speak section. A simple clue to making it more authentic: their words and their emotions are often a mismatch. If not speaking in some form of guy code, it may be that they're simply so uncomfortable with an emotion that they have to come at it sideways.

It's a case of actions speaking louder than words.

Mark seeks out his friend up on an aircraft carrier's PriFly deck. Not because he expects any answers. But because it's chewing at him that Emily Beale was just launched off one of the carrier's catapults and out of his command...and his life.

12

GUY VOICE

I've written a whole book on this topic, *Character Voice: Creating Unique and Memorable Characters*. In it I look at making both male and female characters distinct. Let's briefly look at our male hero.

One of the common failings I see in romance heroes is their voices. They're often indistinguishable from each other.

Do you get feedback, "I can't tell who's speaking?" It can be simple craft, adding *he said / she said* (which personally I rarely use, a purely stylistic choice), action tags, inserting a person's name in the other person's speech, and many other techniques.

Or it could be that the writer has landed on a single *male* voice and used that for all male characters.

Example

Can you imagine these four characters sounding alike:

- Mark: forty-year-old lead-from-the-front commander
- Archie: thirty-five-year-old non-aggressive copilot
- John: thirty-year-old top mechanic
- Tim: thirty-year-old gunner

These are the core male helicopter crew from the first four novels in my The Night Stalkers military romantic suspense series.

Now, let's build them out a bit more with family:

- Mark: Dad was a SEAL
- Archie: Dad was a yacht designer and builder
- John: Oklahoma farming family
- Tim: Rebel from a successful immigrant family

How about a layer of attitudes:

- Mark: pretty unaware of his own emotions, always in control / command
- Archie: highly educated, deeply thoughtful, and aware of his emotions
- John: a joyous storyteller
- Tim: a practical joker

Or one more:

- Mark: itinerant military childhood, parents now settled in Montana (melting-pot father / Cheyenne mother)
- Archie: Boston blue blood (Irish / English)
- John: big boisterous family (black, not the sort of family to use "African American," because they are so rooted in being just American, except for his kick-ass little sister who eventually demanded her own novella)
- Tim: close loving family totally up in each other's lives (Puerto Rican)

Look at how distinct these characters must be, their voices informed by their backgrounds.

Distinguishing Voices

Every factor separates voice. Here are a few:

- Looks (handsome, gawky, self-conscious, handicapped...)
- Age (young, or maybe older but still the youngest on the team, old hand...)
- Family / Team (close, dysfunctional, passive/aggressive, supportive...)
- Occupation (chef, opera singer, corporate magnate, oil rig grunt...)
- Attitude (optimist, pessimist, comedian, observer, controller...)
- Region / Country of origin (by town, state, region, country, culture...)

- Accent (neutral, Texas drawl, clipped Germanic, liquid Latinate...)

I suck at accents. Seriously, I have a total tin ear when it comes to that, a tin ear that carries straight into my writing as well. Knowing that, here's what I did with my four for speech patterns.

- Mark: always aware of the example he's setting, but he whips out a terrible Texas accent when he thinks he's being funny
- Archie: slow-spoken and grammatically correct
- John: boisterous in gesture and speech, and a natural storyteller at every chance (i.e.e. longer paragraphs of speech) always accompanied by dangerously grand gestures
- Tim: short, sharp, wry speech, yet clear and accentless because his immigrant parents would have insisted on that now that they're in America

Playing with It

Now, think about the speech patterns of some of the following and how you'd treat them:

- Young, overconfident, from a big boisterous family, crazy skilled
- A warrior raised as the only kid of a quiet single mom

- A detective raised on MGM musicals
- ...on rock 'n' roll
- ...on opera

If you think the last one is a joke, may I offer the incredibly popular British detective *Inspector Morse* and the follow-on series of his younger days on the force in *Endeavour*. It affects his speech, his attitude, even how he approaches his criminal investigations. For our use, it regrettably also defines his love life...tragic.

A Contemporary Romance Example

Think about these voices. These are from my contemporary romance Where Dreams series set in Seattle (and yes, Seattle also affects their speech and actions).

- The Defender (wealthy fashion photographer from New York)
- The Chatty Italian (brilliant chef, child of a servant in the Defender's NY home)
- The Introvert (Microsoft early retiree)
- The Single Dad Defender (opera stage manager from San Francisco)
- The Easy-going Guy (New York restaurant reviewer turned author)

PART III
PHYSICALITY

13

ATHLETICS

Men are no more naturally athletic than women, but we men are certainly taught how high up athletic skill reigns in the list of essential life skills. The exact opposite rules are applied to women—why weak and demure is considered more attractive than fit and fantastic is something I've never understood. But it was certainly taught to my generation that way. Thank God it's changing.

Men are generally genetically stronger, but more athletically capable? Sorry guys. And as to which is tougher? I have a friend who said "Men get a +1 on strength, but women get a +1 on constitution." If you doubt me, I dare any guy to watch the video of a live birth. Oh. My. God!

I like watching very few sports. Sailing, which is irrelevant here, makes my list. But also Olympic-level gymnastics and diving. Men compete with massive power moves, but the grace and clean lines of the women are equally stunning—different but equally athletic.

The one I find most fascinating to watch is women's volleyball, perhaps because volleyball is one of the few sports I was ever good at.

I learned to play volleyball well during my senior year at college because six of the core members of the women's volleyball team lived in my dorm. Their team was often top of the league (a very low league as we were a small liberal arts college in Maine, but still at the top).

Then there was a campus-wide dorm-versus-dorm intramural volleyball competition. The rule was, there must be at least two members of each gender on every eight-person team. So, the women's team went storming the dorm for two male volunteers. I'd always liked the game in high school gym class and had a decent serve, so I agreed. And once they had us, they spent a lot of hours teaching us two guys how to actually play well. (And they made my serve pretty darn lethal.)

That's when I learned a fascinating difference between how men and women played volleyball. And why I said I watch *women's* volleyball, but not men's.

Men's volleyball is simple—and very fast: serve, save, set, spike. If that spike isn't blocked at the net, it is rarely saved for a return volley. Those spikes are incredibly hard and fast. Not that exciting to watch.

Women's volleyball will become round after round of back-and-forth play before a point is decided—utterly riveting. It's not that women are playing a more intelligent / strategic / cooperative game than their male counterparts. It's only partly that men are taller and more powerful at the spike. It's mostly that the women are willing to throw themselves at the floor to make the dramatic saves and keep the ball in play.

Men, if they don't block the ball right away, will typically drive it to the floor. "We'll overpower them next time," is the operative attitude.

By the end of a game, the women will be black-and-blue and triumphant. I was taught by my college teammates to dive for the floor to make the save. When I joined groups later in life, women would even comment on that difference in my play from most men.

Among men, the spiker is revered. Men are taught the value of power and dominance (both of which I'm personally crap at—especially standing five-foot-six in front of a nearly eight-foot volleyball net and being a lousy jumper). Among women, the setter is the revered one in the more cooperative play, placing that saved ball perfectly for the next attack.

By the way, our team won the collegiate prize. I don't remember if we were given anything, but I remember the feeling of winning as clearly as if it was yesterday rather than forty years ago. The only athletic award I've ever earned.

One final thought on this: is athletic ability truly an indicator of manliness? This is one of those era-based tropes that we need to think about before instilling them into our writing. In my generation, high athletic ability is a standard, perhaps even required, measure of manliness (at which I totally failed and paid the price in bullying).

In Millennials or Gen Z? Sure, some young people are still driven to athletics, perhaps by parents who were raised in an era when it was *de rigueur.* Will they in turn be training their kids that way? Certainly to a far lesser degree than my parents' generation did.

The New Generation

Yep, a nicely arrogant phrase, but bear with me for a moment.

One of the biggest changes I've witnessed is determination. So many of my friends, including me, tumbled out of the back end of high school or college with no clear goals, no idea of what we wanted to do. We're often labeled as the disaffected generation.

My kid is a Millennial. She found her life's work at fifteen and has pursued it relentlessly ever since. So have most of her circle of friends. Sure, they've all smacked into as many barriers and twists in the road as we did, but they consistently formed a far clearer vision than most of my friends ever did.

And I see the escalation continue.

The latest generations seem to pursue everything they do with an almost alarming passion. They don't play soccer, they practice it to the limit. They don't take dance classes, they dance, perform, and excel to levels limited only by their imagination.

See why I said I could never write a modern-day YA novel. How am I of the Boomer Generation, going to dig down inside the emotions of that New Adult? Perhaps, if I taught high school and really listened to them and asked questions...but I don't.

14

PROGRAMMING

I keep coming back to this, and I will more later, because I think it's that important.

Male Heroes

In writing, think very hard about your personal predispositions when writing men. Watch for those automatic biases when you're writing men (or women) characters.

Consider, if you will, popular media's tough male Western culture hero:

- Jason Bourne – silent, grumpy, overtly aggressive
- Jack Reacher – silent, grumpy, overtly aggressive
- James Reece in *The Terminal List* – silent, grumpy, overtly aggressive

- Lorraine Broughton in *Atomic Blonde* – silent, grumpy, overtly aggressive (Charlize Theron kicks ass in a very male-style role, right down to being into women, but at least her character's name doesn't start with a J.)

Realizing this early on, I can only think of one or two heroes that I wrote this way, out of some hundred and fifty.

But there are cultural variations. Consider the media male UK hero:

- Jimmy Perez (*Shetland*) – silent, grumpy, intellectual
- Inspector Morse (*Inspector Morse*) – silent, grumpy, intellectual
- Endeavour Morse *(Endeavour)* – silent, grumpy, intellectual

Of course, the cliché Brit man also brings you soccer riots and notorious pub brawls.

If your male heroes aren't catching fire with your readers, perhaps it's because they sound just like everyone else's.

Genetics

There is also always talk about a male's genetic heritage as a protector-hunter versus a woman's as a nurturer-gatherer. The caveat there is: that dichotomy stopped being true in all but the most obscure places the first moment that grain was planted. Corn, wheat, rice all required intense work and attention but bequeathed a previously unimagined bounty. The days when our ability to throw a spear—at anything other than another human being—mattered, largely disappeared five or ten thousand years ago after we learned to grow our own food.

Recent genetic studies have shown that the human genome has the ability to shift dramatically within mere generations to survive changing conditions. Yet men remain driven by the genetically aggressive hunter mentality?

Personally, my two cents, I think that's at least ninety-nine percent crap.

I will not deny that a man's testosterone-driven physiognomy gives us many opportunities to be stupider than women—definitely upping our aggressive tendencies while it's flooding through our systems. (And women, of course, have no such effects from their own mix of hormones—tongue firmly in cheek but not the point here.)

However, I will posit that these genetic influences are a paltry shadow compared to the social pressures to behave to a certain hand-me-down norm.

I've seen the results of those pressures lessen dramatically across even the generations in the span of my lifetime and I hope the trends continue for a long time to come.

But we're talking about writing. How much of your character's personality is driven by a similar form of genetics—the genetics of what came before you?

If I were to write a hard-core, military-male-driven romantic suspense, would my sales have been higher than what I did write, a military-*woman*-driven romantic suspense?

Perhaps.

Yet I found an audience, one atypically skewed toward women for my genres, that remains riveted by the stories I choose to write. Is your imagined hero's mandate constricting your writing or, even worse, your audience?

Be aware of your male character's genetic heritage—both chemically and driven by the body of prior work in your selected subgenre.

Should you toss out the bad boy, cowboy, knight errant, or ditzy billionaire (who think he knows what he wants but is always proved wrong when he meets the right woman)? Not if you enjoy writing them. Especially not if you find an audience that enjoys the *way* you write about them. Make them richer, more textured and nuanced, and you will build even more reader loyalty.

Afraid of going out on a limb? Allow me to point you at just three reads to get you going:

- *Prince of Midnight,* Laura Kinsale – perhaps the least heroic hero imaginable
- *The Charm School,* Susan Wiggs – the bumbling pirate
- The Ivy Years series by Sarina Bowen – tortured, complex, meek heroes

Just be aware of what you're doing and how the market is shifting.

Class / Culture

How much of this you include is wholly up to you and your awareness of what works—or which battles you choose to fight through fiction. (In my opinion, fiction is perhaps our greatest social transformation tool, another reason I love writing it.) But be aware of the class and culture of your character as well as their "genetic" heritage as you create them.

An emotive, feeling man set in the Pacific Northwest versus set in the Deep South or New England is likely to have been trained very differently by their parents and the society around them.

The same may be true in class levels. Kids of white collar, liberal regions will have been taught to express themselves very differently than say a blue collar inner-city kid, a conservative religious progeny, or a second-generation immigrant family.

For an example, let me use an area I visited thirty years ago. I've heard since that it is little changed.

Fort Collins, Colorado, is the home of the US Air Force Academy and the national headquarters of more than fifty evangelical churches. It is a busy, hard-working, mid-sized city that lies on the flat edge of the Great Plains.

Buried fifteen hundred feet higher in the Rocky Mountains, lies the small town of Manitou Springs. All those years ago, it had an almost commune atmosphere of freedom-loving, intensely liberal, highly educated folks.

The two lie five miles apart.

There's no way, in any generation, that the romantic hero from one of these will express themselves the way the other will. Be aware of your hero's background in class and culture; it will drastically affect their attitudes and use of language.

Speed of Change

And yet one more example.

In the 2000s, Suzanne Brockmann had to fight tooth and nail to publish a novel in which the secondary couple was man-man.

In 2010, my traditional-press editor refused to allow me to write an interracial couple—something I immediately re-included when I recovered the rights to The Night Stalkers #3, *I Own the Dawn*. Why? "Because you've set a white-hetero expectation for your readers with your first two books. If you want to write that, it *must* be under another pen name. You'll alienate your now-established demographic." On book #3. In 2010! *Oy vey!*

By 2014, Sarina Bowen, with only a minor warning for fussier (older) readers, wrote her five-book romance series The Ivy Years with a gay couple for book three. Of course, she did this with her own indie press writing about a generation all of ten years behind the one I was writing about.

In 2022, Miranda Chase, my thriller heroine, eventually decided to take another woman as a lover—after having been with a man for five or six novels. Traditional press, still catering largely to old mindsets, would certainly never have allowed me to do that.

The fact that it worked, because it is true to character for a variety of reasons, wouldn't have mattered. I only received one reader complaint, from a reader self-admittedly in a generation well past mine.

The rules and tropes are changing far faster than mere generations. Keep an eye out for the rules that are in your head.

15

THE MAN'S BODY

This is a crazy-making topic, but I'll do what I can to list a few of the things that I see done inaccurately when writing men in romance novels. And no, I'm not going to be much help to steamy or erotic authors; this book simply isn't going there.

Why is the man's body a crazy-making topic? Because it is one of the easiest places to fall into stereotypes and one of the hardest to avoid. (My copyeditor has threatened to throttle me if I have one more male character crick his neck. As she's my wife, I do pay attention. The Scottish warrior, generally buried deep inside her, definitely rises to the fore when she wields her red pen upon the battlefield of the printed page.)

Above the Shoulders

Yep, there are men out there who practice their smiles in the mirror. (How many women study the hair toss?) Let's just...not talk about those folks. Why? Because they are a cliché of the gender (real or fictional) and we want to dig deeper.

Feel free to *use* the cliché but be aware that you are and, far more importantly, *why* you are. (Guy in the bar restroom will definitely check that his shirt is tucked, his hair isn't a disaster, and might test a quick smile. That's not the same.) If it doesn't fill a specific character purpose, I'd suggest excising it with liberal use of the delete key.

If a guy is meeting a woman's eyes, really meeting them, there's one of two things going on (well, maybe three).

One, he knows that *it's a thing*. It is perhaps the most powerful thing a person of any gender can do to another person, "I see you." A manipulator will definitely use that.

Two, he really does feel the connection. Actually, not quite. It's more likely that he *likes the feeling* of looking her in the eyes, but a typical guy may not be aware of why. He may not understand that's what attraction feels like. He simply likes it. And yep, that's when you hear the line in the bar, "You've got great eyes." (She thinks, "We've been talking for half an hour and he comes up with that lame line *now*?" Not totally lame, perhaps he only just noticed the attraction he was feeling.)

And the oddball third, which I should warn you is at least half me so that means it's way outside the curve, I'll become interested in corneal colors, the shapes of eyebrows, the curve of cheekbones... This isn't quite as weird as I've made it sound. What's actually happening is the guy has made himself uncomfortable, perhaps by simply being attracted and not knowing what to do with that internally, and is unconsciously looking for ways to distract himself from that without quite looking away.

A word on facial hair. Some women say they love a beard, some say they hate it.

So, why do men grow beards and mustaches? For most it's a style statement. But what if it's more than that?

Let's go back to the five whys.

Why did I myself grow a beard while away at college? I wanted to shock my parents.

Why did I keep the beard? Because it absolutely worked when I returned home.

Why did I switch from wild beard to trimmed beard? Because senior year, my best friend's girlfriend (she was awesome but dating my best friend so no chance for me) asked for permission to trim my wild beard for graduation. Afterward she said I looked so much better. That was good enough for me to set a life's pattern.

In midlife I shaved it off for six months but then grew it back. Why? More to remind myself that I wasn't like the lawyers I worked for as a paralegal and IT specialist.

Why Number Five? I still wear my beard, even though my wife finds it rather prickly now that it's gone gray. When I shaved it off five years into our marriage, my chin reminded me of my father. I couldn't grow it back fast enough.

Not only is there depth of *why* behind my beard, there's a changing why across time.

Why does your character have a beard, or not?

Waist to Shoulders

A man sitting with his arm stretched along the back of a seat—or lying across a woman's shoulders with all the charm of a dead fish—is not being an arrogant overly possessive jerk, or maybe not *only* an arrogant overly possessive jerk.

In addition to being a display of male upper body strength, it is also an anatomically very comfortable position for a man. In addition to taking up his manspace, the spread-armed man is also lifting and separating his shoulders, increasing airflow into his lungs (probably not consciously), and feeling better for doing that.

Claiming territory and hoping for an embrace are two more parts of that, of course.

Alternatively, when standing, arms crossed over the chest is almost equally comfortable. When it got labeled as stubborn and aggressive, which it certainly can be, I remember having a hard time shedding my use of that position. I still use it at times when it's just my wife and me chatting. The same effect is achieved by locking fingers behind one's head or neck while leaning back. Again, anatomically very comfortable for a guy.

And jerks are absolutely aware that position also shows off their chest to best advantage.

A woman is taught quite the opposite, both culturally and anatomically.

If she pushes her chest forward, with any gesture, it's *obvious* that she's showing off her breasts or trying to make them look bigger. She *wants it*. Never mind that it might be more comfortable, that's not how a man is going to read such a gesture.

If she hunches forward, it's equally obvious that she's meek and cowering. It has nothing to do with maybe she's attempting to *not* attract every male's attention. Or her bra straps are making her shoulders hurt and she eases forward to relieve the pressure. Yep, a no-win scenario.

Again, I'm just trying to show where female writers of the romantic man go astray. These arm positions aren't *necessarily* arrogant, we are structured differently.

This is also the right time to talk about men's eyes again, even though they're above their shoulders.

For reasons I've never been able to answer satisfactorily for myself or others, and I've asked, a hetero man is going to notice a woman's chest. In fact, he'll probably notice chest, hips, hair, and face—in that order.

I initially became, somewhat desperately, aware of this at that first-ever writer's conference I attended with the many women of the Romance Writers of America. That year, the conference badges had particularly short lanyards. At most conferences, the name tag lands low enough that it is obvious you're looking at someone's name.

However, at that conference, everyone's name tags hung exactly between their breasts. Especially conscious of being one of the few men in attendance, I was never able to look at anyone's name tag—ever. For the most part I had no idea who I'd spoken to at that conference. (It doesn't mean I wasn't aware of how prominently or sleekly that name badge lay, but I sure couldn't look long enough to read the tag *without feeling I was being offensive.)*

The guy who notices shoes, quite likely has altered that order of observation by turning it into a full body scan. Or they may just be really cool shoes. A friend, being a scientist, has very colorful sneakers decorated with the Periodic Table of Elements. A lot of science folks notice, men and women, their eyes caught by the colors and the very distinct pattern rather than because they're doing a toe-to-head body scan. People love her sneakers.

But in general, a guy who doesn't notice shoes is probably just following the first pattern above and carefully not looking down again once his gaze reaches a woman's face. We can be coy, polite, or use our peripheral vision but, trust me, we look and we notice.

I'm not out to make women feel self-conscious, I'm seeking to add realism to your male characters.

I once asked a hetero woman friend in college why she was interested in men and not women because women's bodies were so much more interesting.

"Oh no! A man's body is wonderful. From those nice big shoulders and the way they taper down to his waist and when he's got those tight muscles..." True to her words, she was dating one of the school's top athletes (I'm sure it helped that he was also a seriously nice guy).

Below the Waist

Why do men sit spraddle-legged or with ankle-on-knee crossed legs? He's not just taking up his man space. When he puts his legs together, if he's not careful about the arrangement, he ends up uncomfortable, or even in pain.

Testes trapped between legs and against a hard chair is *not* a comfortable situation. Just sayin'.

Walk Like a Man

Years ago in high school theater, I had a female friend ask me for help. For her drama class, she was doing a part where she had to appear as a man, but later be revealed as a woman.

"Matt, how do I walk like a man?"

Utterly impossible. She was my first major high school crush, though unreachably two years ahead of me, and I had no way to compute the question. But we worked on it one afternoon back and forth across the stage. And I've thought about it plenty since.

There are two primary differences.

First, a guy swings out his foot in a longer stride and plants his heels. Try walking down a steepish slope in hiking boots. Plant the back point of the heel solidly with each step. Then move forward. A man does this even on a flat or somewhat uphill surface with a surety of unconscious power of his right to be there.

Most women who I've observed may step their heel, but not with that outstretched confident thump of declaring their presence. They're far more likely to land flat foot, perhaps to create less noise with their passage. In doubt, try going through the men's and women's shoe section of a thrift store, especially boots and sneakers with the softer soles. Note the wear. Men's shoes get murdered at the heel far faster than women's.

Second, a man's hips remain horizontally stable from side to side. I woman will naturally relax her weight onto each leg as it shifts under her, giving that hip wiggle that everyone makes such a fuss about and that too many girls practice convinced that their body is their primary asset. If you're a woman practicing a man's walk, it will feel painfully stiff. The other way around, the man will discover quite how uptight his hips are; it's very hard to let go.

16

THE FIGHTING MAN

Injury

I'VE NEVER BEEN SHOT, STABBED WITH ANYTHING MORE lethal than a pencil, or had a cut requiring more than seven stitches.

I have talked to guys who have been, and they utterly defy one of the most common tropes in action-romance.

Being badly injured, in any form, you are *not* thinking about sex. Miss America could strip down and offer herself with a smile, and you are *not* thinking about sex. You might admire or ask for a raincheck, but pain meds and bandaging are all that are actually on your mind.

Beaten, battered, hurting? Sure...maybe. Shot, stabbed, bloody? Nope, sorry.

Break this truth in your fiction and you'll knock every male reader (presently estimated at 15-20% of romance readers) right out of the book.

(My proofreader recommends the short, and

presently free, book by Samantha Keel, *10 B.S. Medical Tropes that Need to Die TODAY.*)

On the Run

Does being on the run increase a man's sex drive? He's intact, bad guys are after him, is this the time for a quick shag?

Not quite.

I'll digress for a moment. Twenty years ago a group called the Second Amendment (right to bear arms) Foundation became so disgusted with how firearms were portrayed in novels that they created a course for writers called "Firearms and Fiction." It ran for about five years back in the early 2000s, and I was lucky enough to attend their final year.

The rules were simple: *get to Las Vegas and we'll pay for everything else for two days. Whatever you learn, take it back with you as writers.* Utterly amazing.

The first day was filled with lectures by black belts, the head of forensics of the Las Vegas Police Department, professional military air base security investigators (whose job was to infiltrate our own Air Force bases to identify weaknesses in their defenses), home invasion specialists, and firearms experts.

The second day had three parts.

One: skeet shooting with the women's Olympic gold medalist as a mentor.

Two: at the gun range, loading and firing twenty weapons from a tiny midnight special through an Uzi and an M16 right up to a Barrett M82 sniper rifle that can reach out and touch someone, very permanently, over a mile away with a .50 cal (half-inch) round.

Three: room-clearing in a shoot house. They made this as realistic as possible. Bullet-proof vests and helmets for safety. A handgun loaded with training Simunitions. And a victim and gunman in a four-room plywood structure.

Get the gunman, save the hostage, don't get shot.

We didn't get to see the setup or know what would happen ahead of time. We were led up to the site blindfolded, then it was whipped aside—and all hell broke loose.

The gunman in the doorway, with his arm around the screaming hostage's throat, yelling threats as he dragged her into the shoot house and kicked the door shut.

Adrenaline skyrocketed and there wasn't any room for any other thoughts.

I've talked to trained soldiers. And when they're in it, their focus is absolute in that moment. Their training is more than mere skills. It's about how to still *think* in that environment—analyze and act—but certainly not snuggle off into the corner and have sex while bullets are whistling in through the windows.

Sorry, just not gonna happen.

After the Battle

This is a drastically different question.

Different people reacted in a variety of ways to the shoot-house scenario. I learned as much from witnessing people's reactions as I did from doing the exercise itself.

The one thing this course did very wrong was that they had no after-action counselors. We were a bunch of writers, and some participants were wholly unprepared for their own reactions to the shoot-house experience. A couple of us sort of ended up being group therapists as the twenty different participants tried to each understand their own experience.

There was a distinct gender split here. Many of the women and a few of the men found the exercise to be somewhere between disturbing and terrifying. Perhaps a quarter of the participants, mostly women, couldn't even enter the building.

Most of the balance were more fascinated by their own reaction than shaken up.

A final few rode the adrenal rush for several hours afterward. If someone had offered to have sex with them, they'd have done it in the Las Vegas summer heat up against the splintered back of the shoot house. Every one of them was a man.

Just to complete the story of my reaction during the scenario: I went in. Only later did they tell me that a one-man room-clearing attempt was also called suicide; the gunman has every advantage.

I went wholly...*intellectual*—both during and after.

I eased in low to the first room where the hostage lay screaming in the middle of the floor. In pretend-terror, the hostage attempted to grab me, which would have pinned me in place and made me a static target.

I calculated that if she could still scream that loudly, she was still healthy enough that I had to deal with the shooter to get us out.

But her scream was distracting, so I stopped listening. Literally! To anything. From my point of view, I finished the solo room-clearing in total silence.

When I finally dove into the fourth of the building's four rooms, our gunman-instructor was standing at the front door, facing outward.

I shot him in the back.

He yelped.

Because of my low angle, the Simunition round struck him between the vest and his belt.

Why did he have his back to me?

Because the referee had called out the safe word to end the exercise, but I had stopped listening—to anything.

I was the only person who entered the shoot house who wasn't shot by the gunman, though I'm sure he had several opportunities. I think I also was the only one to get any shot on him…because I kept hunting even after the game had been called off. Oops!

Sex during battle? So not going to happen.

Sex during a car chase or in the middle of a heist? You better build in a quiet moment for it to happen or we simply aren't going to buy in as readers. In the 2000 movie *Gone in Sixty Seconds,* the hero and heroine get very close to having sex in the middle of a car heist. How? Because they're trapped in a car together, but can't start the engine until the owner is too distracted to notice. The moment the owner is out of the picture, the foreplay is gone and the game is back on (much to the hero's frustration). That scenario works.

17

REACTION TYPES

I'VE HEARD IT SAID THAT THERE ARE THREE OR FOUR TYPES of people in a crisis situation, and they aren't always separated by gender.

The Runaway

This is probably the most sensible person. This is the one who sees danger and runs away. Not to get help, but rather to get clear and preserve their own hide.

Watch, if you can bear to, some of the videos when there's a mass shooting. Much of the crowd floods away from the point of danger.

The Freezer

In a moment of crisis, this person won't move—*can't* move.

Many of our group of writers, when exposed to the shoot-house scenario, froze on the spot. In the preparation, we'd been told that it was crucial to rescue the hostage. We *must* do so at any cost. (And you'll be perfectly safe, but it's crucial.)

I think the Freezer is a variation of The Runaway, torn between self-preservation and the instilled need to act. It was an emotionally shredding experience for many of them.

The Call-for-Helper

I had a long talk with someone who convinced me that this was a true category. She witnessed a horrible accident, a train sliced through a truck trailer full of cows stuck on a rail crossing. She had a phone in her hand within seconds. She spoke calmly to emergency services describing the where and what, even finding identifying location information as they'd simply been driving by on a parallel road when it happened.

She didn't move toward or away from the event, not even as the event played out, but she kept her calm and carried on.

The Runner-iner

At the cow accident, her husband didn't even realize what was going on until he was standing by the remains of the truck driver's cab and began helping the man.

At "Firearms and Fiction", each of us who actually entered the shoot house had a significant portion of this in our personal makeup. Many hesitated, some for many seconds before deciding to move forward. I think these were the least affected by the exercise because that hesitation gave them time to distance themselves emotionally from the exercise before engaging.

The very instant the gunman dragged the hostage inside and slammed the door, I was moving forward at an oblique run, angled to stay clear of the door and window as much as possible. I'm told I had the purest runner-iner reaction of the group.

I'm just glad that's never been tested in a real-life situation.

Your Hero

Yep! Nineteen romance heroes out of twenty will be a Runner-iner. I'm not saying that's bad; I'm saying that's a choice you need to make consciously.

What if the crisis isn't guns and accidents?

What if it's the heroine in distress? Or the single-mom's child in danger? Or…

Consider your hero's reactions clearly, then integrate those into the character.

Are they surprised to discover themselves in the middle of the situation? Are they clearly conscious, as I was? Or do they pause long enough to distance themselves emotionally before acting?

Made your choice? Great! Now ask the five whys about what made them that way.

18

THE DNA OF SEX

MUCH OF HOW I THINK ABOUT WRITING COME FROM A single workshop at that 1996 RWA conference: "Crossing Genres" presented by Carole Nelson Douglas, the author of over sixty novels. I'm sad to see that she passed away two years ago so that I can't thank her now that I finally rediscovered who gave that talk. Hats off to you, Carole, and thanks.

My carefully considered question was, "How can I identify if I've written something cross genre, or if it's simply in one genre with some elements of another?" A cross-genre high-fantasy romance will be marketed to a whole different audience than a high-fantasy that happens to have romantic elements.

She had to think about that for several moments before replying, "If you can pull out either element and the story collapses, then it is truly cross genre."

Bang! Not some lazy *Ding!* of a bell or bright flashbulb in my head, but a thunderclap *Bang!* Okay, maybe the bang took a while to propagate to me, like thunder lagging behind the lightning, but it definitely arrived.

Let's look at why.

Vampires

I never wrote a vampire romance, but when I first started thinking about writing romance, the subgenre was unavoidable. Buffy had laid down the roots in 1992 and by the mid-2000s it was hard to touch a romance bookshelf without getting bitten several times.

But what makes some of them work and what makes others die a bloodless death?

That's when I began expanding on Carole's lecture in my head.

"What if instead of pulling an element out and the story collapses, what if I think of it as DNA?" This winds the romance and the vampirishness so tightly together that one doesn't merely support the other: two wooden stakes stuck side-by-side with string tying their tops together. Instead, what if they're inseparably of the same organic construct?

What if each strand of story is an *essential* element of the other?

Another way to think about this is, if you could remove the vampire from the romance and plug in a... race car driver, would the romance still work? If so, it might be cross genre, but it wouldn't be *good* cross genre. The elements must depend upon each other for their very existence.

Military Romantic Suspense (MRS)

So, when I turned my attention to writing MRS a decade after hearing her talk, I still recalled that advice clearly.

MRS is a comingling of three very distinct elements: romance, the suspense factor first given to the heroine by Sandra Brown, and the military element that Suzanne Brockmann had introduced to romance as well. Both women created entire subgenres on their own. Utterly amazing.

In much of MRS, the three coexist, but not much more than that. Peel out the military and put in police and the story still works.

What if I tried to make them so that they *couldn't* exist without each other?

Military: it drives the suspense, but it also is a core factor of the hero and heroine's attitudes, belief structures, and trained skills.

Suspense: it derives from the military events, but it also becomes the key element of the romantic arc pushing and lashing against it at all the wrong—and right—moments.

Romance: the love story could not happen at all if they weren't both military and being driven together and then tested by the specifically military-suspense elements trying to blow them asunder.

To me, that's the DNA of MRS.

DNA of Sex

Then I attempted to apply that same rule to a sex scene.

If I can remove either character and substitute anyone else in their place, then what I have is an erotic moment. A scene of DNA'd sex is when not only could it be no other character, but it must drive the two either together or apart in a way that's *unique* to them.

So many romances, I can page past the sex scene and not miss a thing. Sure, in good writing the emotional relationship will alter before and after sex, but the scene itself may still be skippable.

I read my first three romances—ever—at that 1996 conference. We paged through about fifty more. Several of us sat together one evening and started passing around the scads of free books that were given out at conferences in that day and age.

Read a couple lines, jump thirty pages, read a couple more, jump thirty and—

Oh, their feelings changed, we passed over the first kiss.

Sure enough, there it is. Repeat the process until we'd passed and slipped back to find the sex scene.

Myself and three women in our shared suite—with occasional input from the publisher or one of the other guys—took turns reading out the kiss and sex scenes.

One in ten stood out. Looking back, I now know why. Those authors had, knowingly or by chance, stumbled upon the DNA of sex.

Not only did it have to be *those* two characters. Not only did the act of sex change them. But we *had* to read the sex scene because the author gave us a love scene where we can watch how they were emotionally transformed during the act of sex rather than as a byproduct of it.

That is what I strive for now. Not only in every love scene, but in every scene. What are the twisted-together threads of any scene that makes it unique to those characters involved and that it is absolutely necessary to read?

One reviewer, who became a superfan, complained to me once that I forced her to read too slowly. "Normally I can read a romance novel in a couple of hours, three or four a day when I'm in the mood. Yours I have to read every line or I miss something important."

That's the power of searching for the DNA of the scene, be it a sex scene or not.

PART IV
RELATIONSHIPS

19

THE WHY

HAVING SEX OFFERS A MAN VALIDATION, A SENSE OF POWER, and a brief sense of escape from reality that comes with a mind-blanking release.

But why is he in a relationship?

This almost falls into a Fallacy list, there are a lot of reasons why a guy is in a relationship. The more unique that reason is to your character, the more powerfully your reader will connect to them.

That said, let's look at a few standard reasons anyway. Are these in order of increasing engagement? It depends on the man.

The romance hero, and typically men of at least my generation, won't talk about this, at least not directly. Refer back to the guy-speak section on how they do but don't.

"Why you with her?" "Regular sex." Longish pause, but not long enough to call the stated reason into real doubt. "Uh-huh." Shared wry smiles saying it's so much more than that.

Two good friends may discuss it directly...and briefly—when no one else is around.

Jump to a Millennial, or even a Gen X? The talks about relationships may become long and detailed. A great trend.

Yet I know many who were trained by their silent fathers to share only slivers more. Me personally, despite being a Boomer, I've worked hard to understand my own emotions and how to talk about them—since long before I became a writer. (That, of course, accelerated everything.)

Ease

Sometimes life is simply easier when there are two people.

I'm not talking about it being easy to be with that person. That's an important aspect of a good relationship in my opinion, but it's not my point here. Sometimes, it's literally simply easier.

I rode my bicycle solo around the world as part of an eighteen-month midlife crisis on wheels. I carried my own gear, but I also carried all the gear that might have been split between two people: tent, cooking gear, reading material, repair kits, etc.

During her single-mom period, my wife had to juggle job, kid, food, kid, wood for the heating stove (she was well out in the country), kid... You get the idea. How to keep an eye on the kid, while ax-splitting a cord of wood or mowing the yard could be a nightmare.

Even the least bit participatory partner makes this

easier. By that I mean, a man who crosses the threshold from burden to companion. A guy who leaves the kid, and the wood, *and* the mowing to the mom essentially creates a single mom with two kids. Way worse than being alone.

We were still dating when I unthinkingly carried an armload of firewood inside just to help out. She burst into tears and was a long time recovering enough to explain. Each time I visited and for as long as we lived there, I never again left for work until the wood box was filled.

If the heroine is the chef who typically cooks dinner, there are times when it's nice to simply have someone else cut the blasted vegetables. Or keep the kid safe and entertained while she cooks.

Comfort

The next level is comfort and it's a big one. There are times when life is hard, when the day really, really sucked.

Knowing that you're in a relationship with someone can be very reaffirming, even if you don't talk about the day. *She likes me, puts up with me, whatever. I can't be a total loss of a human being, right?*

Perhaps this last piece forms some of the attraction of the younger trophy wife. If the guy never got much deeper in his personal relationships than his existence being affirmed by whoever stands at his side, perhaps he becomes convinced that he needs that younger, fresher person to affirm his being worthy. Or he's an arrogant jerk who needs to be *the teacher.* Or maybe he just likes showing off what his money can buy.

Companionship

Now we're getting in it a bit deeper.

The man has discovered that he actually *likes* this other person in his life. She's interesting, a challenge, beautiful, whatever it is that drew them together glows richer and deeper in so many good ways.

Partner

Now he has someone to share life's challenges with. To offer advice, to which he might actually listen. Perhaps even to offer actual *thoughtful* advice to his partner.

This is *not* a natural leap in the man's mentality, real or fictional. We're taught that being strong, independent, and reliable are all worthy traits. Thinking about others in any deep way, we naturally want to help them be strong, independent, and reliable. (Assuming we aren't assholes who want to make women weak, reliant, and malleable.)

Therefore, I think it's the man's natural tendency, even at the partner stage, to still aim our partner into our own, predefined-for-us framework of the *best* way—as we perceive it—to be.

The step of partnership past that—listening, thinking, and offering advice that we aren't mortally attached to but is actually just a suggestion—is a next step in which we must train ourselves.

I love seeing the younger generation working on communication, if only to avoid the messes the older generations made of relationships.

You Complete Me / Best Self

Wow is this against the natural (Boomer) male grain. Become *dependent*? Even in a healthy way, on someone else? It is against every bit of cultural education of the modern man, at least the *older* modern man.

I've often said to my wife that, "You aren't on my list, you're the reason I bother to have a list at all." It took her years to believe me because, in her experience with her own generation (same as mine), men simply didn't behave or think that way. I still have to remind her of that truth on occasion—she's awesome just as she is.

Yet "you complete me" has become a worn cliché of its own, falling into codependence or dependence traps.

I'm supposed to rely on someone else for my happiness? The hell you say.

What does it really mean? It means that my wife is the reason I bother to have a list at all. She inspires me to be my best self, and I do my damnedest to offer her the same in return. We call it falling in love with a new person each day. Whatever changes we make in ourselves, the other gets to fall in love with that person too.

20

WHO CHASES WHO

THIS ONE SERIOUSLY CRACKS ME UP.

"I have to wait for the guy to ask me out."

Seriously? What era do you live in? That this was shocking in my generation was bizarre enough. That it persists and a romance heroine still acts that way in this day and age is simply twisted parentage. Of both the author themselves and the characters' heritage within the genre.

There are a lot of underlying factors here.

First, there's always the oblivious man who stumbles into the question, or plunges into it and damn the consequences. But the effect on him will still be much the same.

For real-world guys, "No," may well be the scariest response a man receives—ever. Most guys will go to extremes to avoid the *no*. So scary that he will even twist it, consciously or not, to either mean *yes* or to make it the woman's fault.

He does this instinctively because *no* invalidates his

very manliness in the ways society and culture have trained him to understand. It, almost certainly unconsciously, cuts him to the very quick. For most men, he has already played this conversation out in his head dozens of times. By then he's convinced himself the answer will be yes.

There's a great scene near the end of the 2005 movie *Pride & Prejudice* where Mr. Bingley is to make a final attempt to propose to the girl of his dreams. When doing that utterly fails due to his own nerves getting the better of him? He goes and practices with his good friend Mr. Darcy how to go about a second attempt.

At least to a man, this is far less weird / cute than it looks. It's not that Bingley is a bumbling but sweet man, though he is.

Most men will have a long internal debate about *the ask*—be it a date or marriage—and the ways it might play out. If he really likes the woman, he may well run it by a friend. Not directly, of course. Instead, he'd find ways to test the water and see if the friend thinks the woman is likeable, which implies right away—but thankfully without having to state it aloud—that he's thinking of asking her out.

And then maybe our worried guy will ask the friend, "Who are *you* asking out? How did it go?" or "How did you propose to *your* wife?" Meaning, I want to ask her and I need help on how to do it. Sidling up on the idea is far more comfortable than facing it head-on. Because we don't want that *no* from even our closest friends. "Her? Not a chance, buddy. Totally out of your league." Eek!

How this plays out will vary widely depending upon

your character's level of focus, confidence, fear, and obliviousness.

Women, of course, are all too used to hearing the *no*. It has little power over them (other than probably pissing them off).

Men are convinced that women are deeply mysterious and their actions wholly unpredictable. Personally, I'm convinced of exactly the same thing…and I wish I was closer to half-joking.

Of course, the younger generation men spoil that by actually asking the woman what she's thinking or feeling. I've been told that half the time these guys still think women are confusing as hell and half the time that they're simply people. Even the latter, to this introvert, still makes them deeply puzzling.

In the next section we'll get into a discussion of the hero's journey. Hopefully that will help to answer some of why men feel that way. Any guy who says he understands women is oblivious, lying through his teeth, or has put in enough study to write fifty believable romance novels but still be puzzled by women in real life.

But first we aren't quite done with the man-in-relationship yet.

21

AT BATTLE

When a man fights in a relationship, there are many reactions going on. These can translate directly into your character.

A fight (and we'll stick with non-physical fights) of any ilk will push against the dominant-protector male button like a sledgehammer.

I've come up with five distinct ways that a man typically reacts to an in-the-relationship fight. I've used every one of these in my romances.

Safe Mode

Like battening down a ship's hatches. When he sees the storm coming, he's going to curl up his emotions nice and safe, stow them below, and wait out the storm as best he can.

Getting more than a word or two, or even any out of a man that fights this way is close enough to a miracle to report to the Vatican. The harder he's pushed, the harder he shuts the hell up and locks it all down. He may be furious to the point of his hands shaking—once he's in private—but from the outside it will mostly look stoic.

Asking this guy, "What are you thinking?" gains no traction. "What are you feeling?" No present connection to any feeling except *away*.

In a younger relationship, communication will occur. The brick wall, still prevalent in my generation is fading fast. The communication may be awkward, stilted, confused, emotionally stumbling over his two left feet, but it will occur. That struggle becomes part of the charm of the modern romantic hero—he's trying. He's awful at it, but he's trying.

Superior Mode

This is a jerk-mode fight. One where the didactic "I'm the Voice of God" really thrives in all its blazing gore (not glory).

There will be an absolute insistence of pure rightness that will have nothing to do with reality. A man deeply instilled in his own manliness will simply state truth and ignore everything else thrown at him by the other participant.

And as far as I can tell, the fight never touches him. Why? Because he's right and knows it, even when he's wrong.

I wish it no longer existed; this is the land of the severely passive-aggressive fighter. This is the villain, the over-bearing father, the teacher (who thinks he's a mentor yet will go to his grave insisting he was right all along)...

As a character, this can also be the unreliable narrator who will deny past reality or even flip his position and insist that he never said what he absolutely said before.

Fire and Brimstone

As a fight rains down upon this type's head, he'll heave back as much as he gets or more. He'll go toe-to-toe if necessary to match whatever is coming at him. He'll do this to defend his ego and self-image, right or wrong, because that's what most men have been trained to do.

During the fight, if pushed, he'll let himself say all of those awful things that can never be taken back. They'll lie there and burn holes in the carpet for as long as the relationship survives, even if it's a lifetime.

Afterward, when the blood has cooled, the testosterone subsided, and the attack on his very manliness has been averted, he'll churn on the words. What she said and what he said. Not whatever the fight was about, but rather the nasty shit that they threw at each other that sticks around no matter how you try to wash it out. (Going out and getting drunk with a buddy, doing some stupid driving in a car, or just going out to the wood shop and managing not to cut a finger off are common physical reactions.)

The next part of this is key, and as far as I can tell, always occurs—regret. That regret may turn to self-anger, turn into an apology, or stew up to another fight. But it is the regret that hurts worst on this type of fighter.

Eventually, a bridge can be built over these words heaved at one another, but they'll always be there.

The Fixer

This is me, the guy who will do anything to make it right.

I'll stop the fight, take the blame, admit I was wrong, anything to not be part of the fight. Thankfully, as weird as it may sound, my wife and I don't fight. Why? Because when one of us gets stuck on something, we go to the other and ask for help. Our relationship has been that way since the first day.

The one time I talked myself into a true fury because a whole lot of things out in the wider world were not going well, I came home ready to pick a fight with this absolute red-herring reason burning in my very soul. She simply looked at me and said, "Really? *That's* what's bothering you?"

Uh…nope.

None of what I'd steamed myself up about was relevant. Being laid off, a stiff mortgage with no job meaning the financial burden had just shifted wholly to my wife's shoulders for the time being, and the recent death of my father who I wasn't on speaking terms with even at the end: those were the real issues. Our "fight" was so mild she doesn't actually remember it at all.

Why? Because the instant she pushed back, I utterly folded. That made it easy to shift to reality. The regret of the Fire and Brimstone-style fight never became a factor.

We could go through the whole five whys to figure out

why I'm this way, which I know, but I think it's better if you ask your characters.

The Mis-fight

Like a misfire.

It is the battle about the wrong thing. Much like I would have had in the example above if I'd followed through with my "battle plan."

We'd have had some huge blow-out fight, about *us,* when we weren't the issue. Instead of addressing the external problems together as a team.

For some reason, these seem to be the biggest and loudest fights. It's a form of twisted guy-speak that I've seen a few times in couples. They both know that is *not* what they're fighting about. So, the current fight issue is in a strange way safer.

Rather than regret as an aftermath, here it's typically the worst: burning resentment and buried anger. Why? Because, unlike Fire and Brimstone, it didn't address any real issues. Any regret is buried out of sight beneath the real causes of the fight that were never addressed to begin with.

How does *your* character fight? With silence, didactic superiority, fire and brimstone, the fixer, or coming at it sideways. Every method is unique to your character, if you make it so by instilling their personality and inner motivations into it.

22

THE WEEPING WOMAN

There's a line by Harrison Ford in the movie *Six Days Seven Nights*. "You know how a woman gets a man excited? She shows up. That's it. We're guys, we're easy."

This isn't far wrong. A seriously snuggling hug and a guy is all set and ready for more.

But when confronted with a woman weeping with sadness, there are two distinct reactions that a man might have.

The first, and not inaccurate, depiction? Utter terror.

A man will have absolutely *no* idea at all of what to do with a crying woman. It took me a long time to understand that the woman is rarely looking for the guy to "fix" anything. For them, it is most often about the release of the pain and tears.

Still, it will spook men past reason.

I discovered another version. Over the years, any number of women have found my shoulder to be a comfortable place to let out their sorrow.

As incongruous as it may sound, holding a woman

through that emotional release can make a man feel very strong and powerful. Holding a weeping woman can be an incredibly empowering moment. One crying on each shoulder? Wow! I'm Superman. (This happened in the aftermath of the shoot-house exercise I mentioned before when two friends had been utterly overwhelmed by the experience.)

For the cried-upon man, even when in consoling mode, it is a call to action that he has no tools to answer. His body is supercharged with blood flow and testosterone. Adrenaline has flipped his warrior-protector mode into high gear. And he has not the slightest clue of what to do with all that. The woman can't help him because she's simply being sad.

I learned that the woman simply wants to be held, but for the man it can be an utterly glorious, affirming sensation to be the one providing the comfort—or utterly mortifying.

Hint: if a guy ever cries on a woman's shoulder? He *desperately* wants her to fix it.

PART V
THE JOURNEY

23

THE HERO'S JOURNEY

This has become my super-tool. I use the following concept a lot when building my characters, or when checking them afterward to see how I could improve them during the editing process.

I'm convinced that it's impossible to reach the limits of this tool.

I'm equally convinced that if you plunge right in, you'll end up in that horrid place I mentioned back in the introduction—totally stuck.

There's a lot here. The more you use it, the more you unpack it, the more you'll find you can do with it. Approach it carefully in discrete, well-defined steps, and it should give you immense fun and much richer characters.

Four References

- *The Hero with a Thousand Faces* – Joseph Campbell
- *The Writer's Journey* – Christopher Vogler
- *The Heroine's Journey* – Maureen Murdock
- *The Heroine's Journey* – Gail Carriger

Four quick explanations before we dive in. If you haven't read these books, I cannot recommend them highly enough. We'll delve into them in the most superficial of ways and draw a few romantic conclusions but, if you like the idea of this tool, definitely go read them.

Joseph Campbell spent a lifetime of research unearthing, defining, and teaching the hero's journey from the perspectives of mythology, religion, and cultural anthropology.

Luke Skywalker's character arc through each of the first three original *Star Wars* movies (labeled Episodes IV-VI), and through the three together as a unified arc, follow that hero's journey. Christopher Vogler came along and broke down Campbell's work and laid it out as a storytelling tool with Luke as a pure example.

Maureen Murdock took Joseph Campbell's class about the hero's journey and then asked, "Okay, what's the heroine's journey?" His reply, "She doesn't have a journey, she simply is. She's the reason the hero journeys." This primarily served to tick Murdock off (no surprise there). She spent ten years working as a psychologist for women, then wrote *The Heroine's Journey*.

Thirty years later, Gail Carriger came along and said, "Actually, *that's* the therapy journey for women. *This* is the real heroine's journey."

First, I'll break them down a bit, again, very simplistically.

Hero's Journey (Campbell, Vogler, and Skywalker)

He travels through three main phases, with several steps under each one.

The Ordinary World

- The call to adventure ("Come fight the Empire, Luke.")
- Refuse the call ("I can't. Uncle Owen needs me.")
- Mentor / Call to adventure (Obi Wan drags him away after the Empire offs his aunt and uncle.)

The Adventure

- Tests, allies, and enemies (lot of rescues and battles)
- Getting close to winning...and losing (escalating victories and defeats)
- The Ordeal and Victory (the race between blowing up the Death Star and their own destruction, and Luke's triumphant final shot)

The Return

- Becomes the King (the best of all)

One particular note here, the return to Kingship is a very lonely place to be. The returning hero has outgrown his ordinary world, but the adventure is over and he's now stuck there. Luke gains a sister and a friend. And while he leads as the best of them, he never finds love, has kids, has family. Instead, he ends up alone on an abandoned planet as a real grouch, then dies (sticking with the movie canon and not the written one per an über-*Star Wars*-nerd beta reader).

Heroine's Journey (Murdock)

The Loss

- Embraces the masculine
- Faces trials and challenges
- Achieves the illusion of success

The Awakening

- Aridity of feeling
- Embraces the feminine instead

The Healing

- Blends the masculine and feminine to become whole

Heroine's Journey (Carriger)

Descent

- Broken family network
- Letting go of power and attempts to heal the family

Search

- Hide / Escape
- Surrogate family
- Build a team

Ascent

- Possible reunification with old family network
- Team becomes a new family network, which thrives

Summary

Now let's look at blending these three models together. First, boiling them down to an even simpler form so that we can see how they interact at the most basic level.

- *Hero's Journey:* Leave ordinary world / Adventure / Kingship
- *Heroine (per Murdock):* Loss / Awakening / Healing

- *Heroine (per Carriger):* Descent / Search / Ascent to Family

At this juncture, I'd like to suggest a curious way to use all of this information. In ways that I've had great fun with, and that absolutely fits the male hero stereotype while making your character vastly richer and deeper.

Let's take these three summarizations and edit them a little.

- *The Hero's EXTERNAL Journey:* Leave ordinary world / Adventure / King
- *The Hero's INTERNAL personal journey (per Murdock):* Loss / Awakening / Healing
- *The Hero's INTERNAL family journey (per Carriger):* Descent / Search / Ascent to Family

The story now becomes:

- Leaving the ordinary world, losing a sense of self, and losing family (the lonely hero embarking on a romantic adventure, probably without realizing it)
- Plunging into the adventure (meeting the woman), awakening to his own feelings, and searching for more of that
- Triumphant return (to a self he never probably knew) and wins family and a happy ever after

This is the ultra-compressed version. Now? Start expanding your story on top of it. I have yet to find a romantic subgenre this can't be applied to. It has even served me well in science fiction romance. Here's a contemporary romance example:

Wildly successful New York fashion photographer burned out on his work. Why? He has ended up turning completely commercial for the only clients who could still afford him. He's gone completely cold. He doesn't even feel anything for the supermodel in his bed.

His best friend is a chef in Seattle. In adventuring there, he has several scrapes, including meeting the heroine he can't stand. But he also discovers sailing, wholly unaware that it's the freedom he appreciates as he searches for something to do (actually searches for himself).

When he realizes that the woman of his dreams is another side of the woman making him crazy, he awakens enough to remove his ego and makes the ultimate sacrifice; he leaves her so as to not block her illustrious future.

She's been on her own internal journey through all this, and realizes that in embracing all of those male-sanctioned goals (per Murdock), she too has abandoned herself.

Upon facing the ultimate challenge, they heal themselves, he returns as the king who has learned and grown, and together they thrive in a family network of friends and each other.

This is the hero's journey of Where Dreams #1, *Where*

Dreams Are Born, a contemporary romance series that I set in Seattle.

Want more ideas? Read the four books at the head of this chapter, there are a lifetime's worth of ideas there.

24

THE MODERN HERO'S JOURNEY

I'VE PUT WARNINGS THROUGHOUT THIS BOOK ABOUT BEING conscious of your era. So, let's look at three of the greatest *modern* heroes and peek at their journeys very briefly. None are a romance at the heart of the story, but they're great examples of how to manipulate this tool.

Harry Potter and Katniss Everdeen and Aang.

Note: I'm using Harry because he and his journey are so well known in print and film across generations. For the purposes of this book, like Mark Owen in *No Easy Day* in the reference section, I'm only interested in the writing and the character.

Harry Potter

Unlike Luke or any of my own era heroes, Harry is *painfully* aware of his own thoughts, feelings, and emotions. Yet he follows much of the hero's path, though not all of it.

- *The Call to Adventure* ("You're a wizard, Harry."): He leaves the ordinary world with minimal hesitation.
- *The Adventure:* He has many ever-escalating challenges (seven books' / eight films' worth).
- *The Return:* He returns as the king, the greatest wizard of the age. But he turns down the mantle to raise his family (Carriger's heroine's journey) as a worker at the Ministry of Magic.

Katniss Everdeen, *The Hunger Games*

Unlike Harry, Katniss is never connected to most of her emotions, only to her anger and pain.

- *The Call to Adventure:* She is forced on the adventure, in an attempt to heal and save her failing family. Like Harry, she does this without hesitation.
- *The Adventure:* She must embrace the lethality of the manly adventure to return triumphant. Yet each victory is as hollow as Murdock predicted because the game is rigged. She ultimately becomes both the King Slayer and the King Maker.
- *The Return:* Only in the last few scenes of Book #3 (Movie #4) does she embrace any actual healing and positive emotion. A very select chosen family per Carriger.

Aang, *Avatar: the Last Airbender* (the anime, not the blue people)

This 2005-2008 animated series was a global phenomenon to younger generations and almost wholly unknown to mine (my kid suggested it when I was studying the YA voice).

Aang speaks freely of his emotions and confers with his cohorts and perhaps best embodies all three of the journeys in combination.

- *The Call to Adventure:* He resists, encasing himself and his sky bison in Antarctic ice to escape genocide. He is unfrozen after the war that has killed all of his race. He accepts the adventure to restore balance to the world.
- *The Adventure:* Many trials and tribulations, gaining and losing companions. He even dies, but is restored to continue the challenge of bringing peace and balance to the world.
- *The Return:* With his found family, he reigns triumphant, overcoming race hatred, totalitarianism, and proving that freedom of choice is the true power. He saves the world, restoring balance, with no need to rule, instead thriving with his found family. He also embraces his own power to join the others in the challenge of healing the world.

These are very different tales, where the authors

(consciously or not) are manipulating this overlapping pattern of journeys to their own ends to create amazingly deep and engaging characters.

PART VI

THE FINAL BITS

25

MEN IN ROMANCE

A few random thoughts

- Guys *have* emotions, however, typical men are *NOT* practiced in understanding or communicating them. And the fear of the "No" will often make even the most erudite of them hesitate or choose silence.
- Real-life guy traits exist. But ask yourself, as you use them in fiction, if they are relevant to your characters and your writing. If they are, drill into the five whys to discover their underlying motivations.
- Guys are trained from birth to make sure they're the best. If they can't strive upward, they'll strive downward. For years, I always made sure that I won the one-downsmanship contest. "Your boss does that, well, my boss does this." "Your father was like that, mine

was…" "She dumped you for someone nicer? Well, let me tell you about being dumped. This amazing woman said to me as she walked away…" That was a contest that took me a long time to stop trying to win, even after I learned how self-destructive it was. Yet I still hear it around me all the time by guys trying to "win" the game.

- A guy will talk about himself very easily. Perhaps out of supreme arrogance, but also perhaps due to having no bleeding clue what else to do, like ask the lady a question.
- Neat freak or slob? Ask yourself the five whys to dig down into something richer than, "Because he's as mature as a teenager?" Perhaps… "My dad was a slob in protest against his parents until he joined the Navy. Part of the Navy safety discipline included occasional visits to the cabin by an officer wielding a firehose; anything not properly stowed was washed overboard. Ever since, he would tolerate a book left out, if you were actively reading it, but not two."

Avoiding the "woman's perspective" in your writing of men

- Skip cliché.
- Avoid the quarter-round hero. Multi-dimensional is always the answer to this.

- Be consistent with a character's past and *ALL* of their present.
- There are jerks, misogynists, narcissists...but ask the character *Why* to get depth.
- Practice your guy-speak, especially the mismatch of thoughts vs. emotions.
- Have fun, because your audience can *always* tell if you did.

Questions?

Or want to send in a guy trait, visit my website at https://mlbuchman.com and fill out the form at the end of the About / Contact page. I'd love to hear from you.

OTHER STRATEGIES FOR SUCCESS TITLES

Available at mlbuchman.com
and fine retailers everywhere.

Managing Your Inner Artist/Writer
Strategies for Success

M.L. BUCHMAN(S)
Two Artists Engaged in Their Art

ESTATE PLANNING FOR AUTHORS
*Your Final Letter
(and why you need to write it now!)*

M.L. BUCHMAN
Strategies for Success

CHARACTER VOICE
Creating Unique and Memorable Characters

M.L. BUCHMAN
Strategies for Success

NARRATE AND RECORD YOUR OWN AUDIOBOOK
a simplified guide

M. L. BUCHMAN
Strategies for Success #4

ABOUT THE AUTHOR

USA Today and Amazon #1 Bestseller M. L. "Matt" Buchman started writing on a flight south from Japan to ride his bicycle across the Australian Outback. Just part of a solo around-the-world trip that ultimately launched his writing career.

From the very beginning, his powerful female heroines insisted on putting character first, *then* a great adventure. He's since written over 70 action-adventure thrillers and military romantic suspense novels. And more than 125 short stories, and a fast-growing pile of read-by-author audiobooks.

PW declares of his Miranda Chase action-adventure thrillers: "Tom Clancy fans open to a strong female lead will clamor for more." About his military romantic thrillers: "Like Robert Ludlum and Nora Roberts had a book baby."

His fans say: "I want more now...of everything!" That his characters are even more insistent than his fans is a hoot. He is also the founder and editor of *Thrill Ride – the Magazine.*

As a 30-year project manager with a geophysics degree who has designed and built houses, flown and jumped out of planes, and solo-sailed a 50' ketch, he is awed by what is possible. He and his wife presently live on the North Shore of Massachusetts. More at: www.mlbuchman.com.

Other works by M. L. Buchman: (* - also in audio)

Action-Adventure Thrillers

Dead Chef
One Chef!
Two Chef!

Miranda Chase
*Drone**
*Thunderbolt**
*Condor**
*Ghostrider**
*Raider**
*Chinook**
*Havoc**
*White Top**
*Start the Chase**
*Lightning**
*Skibird**
*Nightwatch**
*Osprey**
*Gryphon**

Science Fiction / Fantasy

Deities Anonymous
Cookbook from Hell: Reheated
Saviors 101

Contemporary Romance

Eagle Cove
Return to Eagle Cove
Recipe for Eagle Cove
Longing for Eagle Cove
Keepsake for Eagle Cove

Love Abroad
Heart of the Cotswolds: England
Path of Love: Cinque Terre, Italy

Where Dreams
Where Dreams are Born
Where Dreams Reside
*Where Dreams Are of Christmas**
Where Dreams Unfold
Where Dreams Are Written
Where Dreams Continue

Non-Fiction

Strategies for Success
Managing Your Inner Artist/Writer
*Estate Planning for Authors**
Character Voice
*Narrate and Record Your Own Audiobook**

Short Story Series by M. L. Buchman:

Action-Adventure Thrillers

Dead Chef

Miranda Chase Stories

Romantic Suspense

Antarctic Ice Fliers

US Coast Guard

Contemporary Romance

Eagle Cove

Other

Deities Anonymous (fantasy)

Single Titles

The Emily Beale Universe
(military romantic suspense)

The Night Stalkers
MAIN FLIGHT
The Night Is Mine
I Own the Dawn
Wait Until Dark
Take Over at Midnight
Light Up the Night
Bring On the Dusk
By Break of Day
Target of the Heart
Target Lock on Love
Target of Mine
Target of One's Own
NIGHT STALKERS HOLIDAYS
Daniel's Christmas*
Frank's Independence Day*
Peter's Christmas*
Christmas at Steel Beach
Zachary's Christmas*
Roy's Independence Day*
Damien's Christmas*
Christmas at Peleliu Cove

Henderson's Ranch
Nathan's Big Sky*
Big Sky, Loyal Heart*
Big Sky Dog Whisperer*
Tales of Henderson's Ranch*

Shadow Force: Psi
At the Slightest Sound*
At the Quietest Word*
At the Merest Glance*
At the Clearest Sensation*

White House Protection Force
Off the Leash*
On Your Mark*
In the Weeds*

Firehawks
Pure Heat
Full Blaze
Hot Point*
Flash of Fire*
Wild Fire

SMOKEJUMPERS
Wildfire at Dawn*
Wildfire at Larch Creek*
Wildfire on the Skagit*

Delta Force
Target Engaged*
Heart Strike*
Wild Justice*
Midnight Trust*

Emily Beale Universe Short Story Series

The Night Stalkers
The Night Stalkers Stories
The Night Stalkers CSAR
The Night Stalkers Wedding Stories
The Future Night Stalkers

Delta Force
Th Delta Force Shooters
The Delta Force Warriors

Firehawks
The Firehawks Lookouts
The Firehawks Hotshots
The Firebirds

White House Protection Force
Stories

Future Night Stalkers
Stories (Science Fiction)

SIGN UP FOR M. L. BUCHMAN'S NEWSLETTER TODAY

and receive:
Release News
Free Short Stories
a Free Book

Get your free book today. Do it now.
free-book.mlbuchman.com